POLITICAL PARTIES

AND

THE CONSTITUTION

Other Titles in this Series:

POLITICAL PARTIES
AND THE CONSTITUTION

by Michael Les Benedict

Published by the
American Historical Association
400 A Street, SE
Washington, D.C. 20003
www.historians.org

and sponsored by the
Institute for Constitutional History
at the New-York Historical Society
and the George Washington University Law School

ABOUT THE AUTHOR

MICHAEL LES BENEDICT is an emeritus professor of history at Ohio State University, the parliamentarian for the American Historical Association, and a member of the AHA's Task Force on Intellectual Property. Benedict received his B.A. and M.A. degrees from the University of Illinois and his Ph.D. from Rice University. He has contributed several crucial works to the field of Civil War and Reconstruction studies, including The Impeachment and Trail of Andrew Johnson (1973), A Compromise of Principle: Congressional Republicans and Reconstruction, 1863-1869 (1975), Fruits of Victory: Alternatives in Restoring the Union, 1865-1877 (1986), and Preserving the Constitution: Essays on Politics and the Constitution in the Reconstruction Era (2006). He is also the author of The Blessings of Liberty and other works on American constitutional history.

© 2015 by the American Historical Association
ISBN: 978-0-87229-042-6

Published in 2015 by the American Historical Association. As publisher, the American Historical Association does not adopt official views on any field of history and does not necessarily agree or disagree with the views expressed in this book.

Benedict, Michael Les.
    Political parties and the Constitution / by Michael Les Benedict.
        pages cm — (New essays on American constitutional history series)
        "Sponsored by the Institute for Constitutional History at the New-York Historical Society and the George Washington University Law School."
    Includes bibliographical references.
    ISBN 978-0-87229-042-6
    1. Political parties—United States—History. 2. Constitutional history—United States. I. Title.
    JK2261.B447 2015
    324.273—dc23   2015029379

TABLE OF CONTENTS

SERIES INTRODUCTION

New Essays on American Constitutional History is published by the American Historical Association, in association with the Institute for Constitutional Studies. This series follows the lead of its predecessor, the Bicentennial Essays on the Constitution, published by the AHA under the editorship of Herman Belz as part of the commemoration of the two hundredth anniversary of the Constitution over two decades ago. The goal remains the same. The essays are intended to provide both students and teachers with brief, accessible, and reliable introductions to some of the most important aspects of American constitutional development. The essays reflect the leading scholarship in the field and address topics that are classic, timely, and always important.

American constitutionalism is characterized by a series of tensions. Such tensions are persistent features of American constitutional history, and they make a frequent appearance in these essays. The American tradition emphasizes the importance of written constitutions. The United States Constitution declares that "this Constitution" is the "supreme law of the land." But time moves on. Politics and society are ever changing. How do we manage the tension between being faithful to a written constitutional text and adapting to changing political circumstances? To the extent that the American brand of constitutionalism binds us to the past, creates stability, and slows political change, how do we balance these conservative forces with the pressures of the moment that might demand departures from inherited ways of doing things and old ideas about rights and values? We sometimes change the terms of the old text through amendment or wholesale replacement of one constitution with another (from the Articles of Confederation to the Constitution at the national level, or more often at the state level), but we apply and adapt the inherited constitutional text through interpretation and practice. All the while, we manage the tension between being faithful to the text that we have and embracing the "living constitution" that grows out of that text.

Law figures prominently in the American constitutional tradition. Our written constitutions are understood to be fundamental laws and part of our legal code. They are the foundation of our legal system and superior to all other laws. They provide legally enforceable rules for judges and others to follow. Judges and lawyers play an important role in interpreting American constitutions and translating the bare bones of the original text into the detailed body of doctrine known as constitutional law. It has often been the dream of judges, lawyers, and legal scholars to insulate constitutional law from the world of politics. There is a long-held aspiration for judges and lawyers to be able to spin out constitutional law in accord with established principles of justice, reason, and tradition. But politics has also been central to the history of American constitutionalism. Constitutions are created by political actors and serve political purposes. Once in place, constitutional rules and values are politically contested, and they are interpreted and put into practice by politicians and political activists, as well as by judges. The tension between law and politics is a persistent one in American constitutional history.

A final tension of note has been between power and liberty. In the modern tradition, constitutional government is limited government. Constitutions impose limits and create mechanisms for making those constraints effective. They specify what the boundaries of government power are and what rights individuals and groups have against government. But there is also an older tradition, in which constitutions organize and empower government. The U.S. Constitution contains both elements. Many of its provisions, especially the amendments, limit government. These are some of the most celebrated features of the Constitution, and they have become the basis for much of the constitutional law that has been developed by the judiciary. But the Constitution was specifically adopted to empower the federal government and create new, better institutions that could accomplish national objectives. Both the U.S. Constitution and the state constitutions are designed to gather and direct government power to advance the public good. Throughout American constitutional history, judges, politicians, and activists have struggled over the proper balance between empowering government and limiting government and over the best understanding of the rights of individuals and the public welfare.

These essays examine American constitutionalism, not a particular constitutional text. The U.S. Constitution figures prominently in these essays, as it does in American history, but the American constitutional tradition includes other foundational documents, including notably the state constitutions. These texts are a guide to the subject matter of these essays, but they are not exhaustive of it. Laws, court decisions, administrative actions, and custom, along with founding documents, perform constitutional functions in the American political system, just as they do in the British system where there is no single written "constitution." Whether "written" or "unwritten," constitutions perform certain common tasks.

Constitutions define the organic structures of government, specifying the basic institutions for making and implementing public policy, including the processes for altering the constitution itself. Constitutions distribute powers among those institutions of government, delegating, enumerating, prohibiting, and reserving powers to each governmental body. The flip side of entrusting power and discretion to governmental bodies is the definition of limits on those powers, the specification of individual and collective rights. Constitutions also specify who participates in the institutions of government and how and to whom the power of government applies. That is, constitutions identify the structures of citizenship and political jurisdiction. Across its seven articles and twenty-seven amendments, the U.S. Constitution addresses all of these topics, but the text is only a starting point. These topics form the subject matter of New Essays on American Constitutional History.

Writing early in the twentieth century, the great constitutional historian Edward Corwin observed that relatively few citizens actually read the U.S. Constitution, despite its brevity. He thought that this was in part because the "real constitution of the United States has come to mean something very different from the document" itself. The document laid out the framework of government, but "the real scope of the powers which it should exercise and of the rights which it should guarantee was left, to a very great extent, for future developments to determine." Understanding American constitutionalism requires understanding American constitutional history. It is a history of contestation and change, creation and elaboration. These essays aim to illuminate that history.

—Keith E. Whittington,
Princeton University

—Gerry Leonard,
Boston University School of Law

INTRODUCTION

Political parties are central to the American constitutional system, yet the Constitution itself nowhere mentions them. To understand their role and the way they are affected by the Constitution, one has to look beyond the document, for our constitutional system consists of much more than the written Constitution. The Constitution provides the foundation, but the constitutional system includes the institutions, customs, and interpretations that are fundamental to it. An important part of the Constitution outside the document is the legal interpretation of its languages and principles articulated by judges in courts. This interpretation forms the heart of *constitutional law.*

We also have what may be called *constitutional customs.* These are long-standing practices that have become part of the system. For example, although the Constitution requires only that heads of executive departments provide written opinions to the president at his request, the president has treated the heads of executive departments as a "cabinet" of formal advisers ever since George Washington established the practice. In 1939 Congress established the Executive Office of the President (EOP), which has grown to consist of numerous offices and councils that overlap the traditional executive departments, often displacing them as sources of information and advice. Neither the cabinet nor the EOP are mandated by the Constitution or by constitutional law, but no description of the American Constitution would be complete without their inclusion. Nor does the Constitution mandate the existence of political parties. In fact, the framers thought them a danger to republican government. Yet they are an essential element of the constitutional system, performing important constitutional functions. There are also statutes that are so fundamental that they may be called part of the customary Constitution, such as the Social Security Act. Their terms may be changed, but repealing them would require a fundamental shift in how Americans regard government.[1]

Many policies that carry out constitutional mandates are devised outside the courts. The president, Congress, the state legislatures and governors, and even local officials enact laws and undertake actions that protect our constitutional rights. They establish the courts and administrative agencies that assure we won't be deprived of life, liberty, or property without due process of law. They pass laws and create agencies to combat racial, gender, religious, and ethnic discrimination. At the same time, their actions also constrain our rights. They regulate our behavior in any number of ways and limit what we can do with our property.

Public officials take oaths to support the Constitution of the United States and their state constitutions, so they are required to make judgments about whether proposed actions are constitutional. This involves what political scientist Keith Whittington calls "constitutional construction"— "elaborating constitutional meaning in the political realm."[2] Public officials have fulfilled this obligation over most of our history, although they have been less diligent since the 1950s and 1960s, deferring more and more to the Supreme Court. Our public servants can refuse to enact programs they believe would violate constitutional principles—in effect, determining their unconstitutionality before judges ever get a chance to evaluate them. There are some inherently constitutional issues, such as the grounds for impeaching federal officers, that courts have never been willing to take up. Likewise, judges have always been reluctant to intervene in disputes between the other branches of the federal government. In all these areas, political actors representing the American people make constitutional policy, even if they do not make constitutional law. Constitutional politics plays an important role even where Americans concede that Supreme Court justices make final decisions. Americans can use the political process to put immense pressure on judges if judgments seem to diverge to greatly from popular understandings of what the Constitution means.[3] As another political scientist has observed, "Constitutional politics in the United States extends beyond the practice of judges enforcing fundamental norms . . . . It is also a function of commitments and actions within the polity at large."[4]

Viewed from a broad perspective, all these elements of the American constitutional system, even constitutional law, are products of constitutional politics—the way in which people promoting and protecting their interests make constitutional arguments to secure their goals, and the way others respond to them. Constitutional politics are shaped and constrained by the institutions to which they are addressed and through which they are articulated. Political parties are among the most important of those institutions. They have played a critical part in this process. In fact, our parties first organized over disagreements about what the Constitution meant. Constitutional issues remained at the heart of party differences through much of the nineteenth century, and differences over constitutional interpretation remain important markers of party identification today.

At the same time, the Constitution has affected the organization and practice of political parties. As their constitutional importance has become clear, they have evolved from private associations of citizens, unregulated by law, to highly regulated quasi-state institutions. Yet the courts have interpreted the Constitution's guarantees of free speech and freedom of association to limit the regulations that the state and federal governments may impose.

In sum, one cannot understand the American Constitution without understanding the role political parties have played in shaping it, and the Constitution, in turn, has played a reciprocal role in the development of political parties. The following essay surveys the origins of political parties in the United States and the Founders' attitudes toward them (Chapters I and II); the way parties articulated rival constitutional principles afterward (Chapter III); other functions that parties have served in the constitutional system (Chapter IV); and the way the Constitution has influenced the development, organization, and regulation of parties (Chapter V).

I. The Founders and the Evils of Parties

T he founders of the United States were deeply suspicious of parties, and "anti-partyism" has competed with party loyalty among Americans ever since. In the end, however, the structure of government inaugurated under the Constitution seems to require parties in order to operate.

Parties as a Danger to Republican Government

At the time Americans declared their independence from Great Britain and founded the United States, most considered party spirit inimical to good government. In 1763, a young John Adams swore he would never "wound my own mind by engaging in any party, and spreading prejudices, vices, or follies." As late as 1796, in his *Farewell Address* upon leaving the presidency, George Washington warned Americans against "the baneful effects of the Spirit of Party."[5]

The purpose of government, Americans believed, was to serve the common good and preserve liberty. In monarchies like Britain's, liberty and the general welfare were always threatened by the king and aristocrats—a "court party" that always perverted government to promote its leaders' selfish interests and inflated ambitions. The effort to tax Americans without their consent was only the most recent in a long line of ministerial subversions of liberty. Americans determined to assure liberty by substituting republican for monarchical government. In a republic the people would select leaders dedicated to the general welfare, free of the corrupting influence of a king and aristocrats. But history taught that liberty could be endangered in republics too. Ambitious men would seek power by appealing to the special interests of the few at the expense of the good of the whole. These special interests and ambitions were the source of "party" and "faction." Factions and parties led to disputes, disorder, and oppression. They were the particular bane of republics—"truly their worst enemy," Washington said—and had often led citizens to abandon the enterprise. James Madison expressed the universal concern: "The friend of popular governments never finds himself so much alarmed for their character and fate as when he contemplates their propensity to this dangerous vice."Only a people of great self-discipline—a "virtuous" people, in the language of the day—could resist the blandishments of demagogues and govern themselves through a republic. In the words of American revolutionary General Charles Lee, it required "a public and patriotick spirit reigning in the breast of every individual superceding all private considerations."[6]

The Constitution against Parties

Americans were dismayed when factions appeared in every state even before the Revolution ended. Especially troubling was that these divisions showed that factions did not necessarily consist only of minorities seeking special privileges. Most of the leaders of the Revolution were especially appalled as debtor factions in many states pressed for laws to relieve their distress. As voters elected legislatures that responded to the debtors' demands, it became clear that a faction could consist of a majority that had lost sight of the general good. A disillusioned Lee wrote that he now believed republican liberty "could be only supported by qualities not possess'd by individuals in the modern world." Washington lamented, "[N]otwithstanding the boasted virtue of America, we are far gone in every thing ignoble and bad."[7] Convinced that dedicated men of integrity could distinguish the public interest from special interests, few if any Americans yet perceived that honest men could disagree systematically about what the public interest was and how best to serve it.

Although the Constitutional Convention of 1787 was called primarily to strengthen the general government, the question of how to counteract factionalism and party was among the framers' most urgent concerns. The most influential delegates now doubted that they could rely on public virtue alone to combat the threat. So they attempted to establish a system of government that would diminish the danger. As Alexander Hamilton put it, "We are attempting by this Constitution to abolish factions and to unite all parties for the general welfare."[8]

They did it in a number of ways. They shifted issues that had stirred factionalism in the states to the central government. Then they tried to "filter" potential leaders of the federal government for integrity and ability by having one group of elected officials elect a higher-level group. State legislatures would elect United States senators. Presidential "electors" would elect the president. If no one was the choice of a majority of the electors, the House of Representatives would choose from among the five leading vote-getters, with each state delegation casting a single vote. The candidate who came in second would be vice president.

The framers also hoped that a government for the whole country would be more impervious to factions than state and local governments were. Electoral districts would be large. The framers expected that it would take a greater degree of prominence and respectability to secure election from such districts. To prevent any faction or coalition of factions from gaining control of all the institutions of government, they divided authority, first between the state and federal governments and then within the federal government itself. They separated the government into legislative, executive, and judicial branches. They divided the legislature into two houses. Then they gave each part of the government power to obstruct the other parts. Election cycles were staggered so representatives, senators, and the president were never all elected at the same time. Federal judges received tenure for life. Each branch was given an opportunity to check and balance the actions of the others—each house of Congress could reject a bill passed by the other; the president could veto proposed laws; the houses of Congress would have to act together to override the vetoes; the Senate had to confirm presidential appointments and ratify treaties the president negotiated.

These checks and balances meant that government would require consensus. With power so fragmented, proposals to promote selfish and special interests surely would be frustrated at one point or another, the framers thought. Only proposals that served the general interest could garner enough support to run the gauntlet. Hopefully, all these elements would lead to the selection of public officials most likely, in delegate James Madison's words, "to discern the true interest of their country, and . . . least likely to sacrifice it to temporary or partial considerations." Of all the advantages the Constitution offered, Madison wrote, the most important was "its tendency to break and control the violence of factions." It provided "a republican remedy for the diseases most incident to republican government."[9] So it is not surprising that the Constitution did not refer to parties at all, and that various provisions proved almost unworkable once parties developed.

II. The Persistence of Party: Federalists and Jeffersonian Republicans

The framers had hoped that establishing a national government would diminish the importance of factions and parties. Instead, nationalizing the government led to nationalized parties. Important issues would now be settled at the national level, and like-minded people in all the states began to cooperate to secure their interests and promote their notions of the public good. The disputes that divided them were closely tied to different interpretations of the Constitution itself. [10]

Alexander Hamilton, Washington's Secretary of the Treasury, precipitated the conflict by proposing measures that linked the federal government to economic development. He urged the incorporation of a national bank with branches around the country. He suggested taxes (or "tariffs") on foreign imports, not only to raise money for the government but to encourage the development of American industries. To many Americans, Hamilton's program smacked of the kind of policies corrupt British "court" parties had used to buy political support for their ministries. Hamilton himself did not disguise his desire to align the interests of the rich and powerful with the federal government.

Hamilton's opponents organized around the constitutional ideas expressed by Secretary of State Thomas Jefferson and James Madison, now a leader in the House of Representatives. Unwilling to concede they were building a party, they claimed to represent the "republican interest" of the country. In a widely circulated paper addressed to President Washington in February 1791, Jefferson pronounced Hamilton's scheme for a national bank unconstitutional.[11] It exceeded the powers that the Constitution delegated to the federal government, he insisted. Federal power should be interpreted strictly, lest it break down the boundaries the Constitution established between state and federal jurisdiction.

---

* The Jeffersonian Republican Party should not be confused with the modern Republican Party, which was founded in 1855. The modern-day Democratic Party claims to be the heir of the Jeffersonian Republicans, who sometimes called themselves Democratic-Republicans.

Jefferson's principles of "state rights" and "strict construction" of federal power became the foundational principles of Jefferson and Madison's Republican Party.*

Hamilton responded in an equally influential opinion to Washington. While limited to the exercise of delegated powers, the federal government was supreme within its sphere of authority, he insisted, with the same broad, sovereign powers as any other national government.[12] The principles of national sovereignty and broad construction of federal power became the cornerstones of Hamilton's Federalist Party.

Although powerful economic interests lined up for and against Hamilton's policies, the arguments were made largely in constitutional terms. These had been the terms in which British politics, including those in the colonies, had been articulated for generations. Rival interests and politicians were accustomed to seeing themselves as defending constitutional principles, and they were the most powerful arguments with which to attract the support of those who did not share the particular interests at stake. It was not enough for Hamilton to convince people that a bank was beneficial if Jefferson could persuade them it was unconstitutional.

Soon Jefferson, Madison, and others were in open opposition to the Washington administration, although they carefully avoided attacking the beloved president himself. Sympathizers organized Democratic Societies, which Federalists denounced as "political machines which fatal experience . . . has proved to be the destroyers and tyrants of the people."[13] Partisans held parades, waved banners, organized clubs, attended banquets where they toasted their principles and leaders, read newspapers that favored their side and sang (or at least read the lyrics of) songs printed on the back page.[14] When Washington retired, Adams and Jefferson were the consensus candidates of the rival political alliances. Adams won the most votes from the presidential electors. It was a sign that these alliances were not yet firmly disciplined that Jefferson came in second and thus became vice president. It was an anomaly in an increasingly partisan system, but it was a logical result of an election procedure that supposed electors would vote for men, not parties.

By no means complete political organizations, the Federalist and Republican "interests" were nonetheless recognizable parties They were alliances of politicians who shared common principles—especially constitutional principles—and articulated those principles to a broader public whose political support they sought. Influenced by Hamilton, Washington appointed those who shared Federalist views to federal offices, a policy Adams continued.

The differences extended into the states. There the Republican watchwords became "equal rights and no special privileges." They moved to end the special privileges accorded established churches in some of the states. They opposed giving corporate charters to influential businessmen. They demanded that the right to vote be extended and that seats in state legislatures be more fairly apportioned.[15] Federalists saw these propositions as dangerous demagoguery. Their concern grew as Republicans expressed sympathy for the ever more radical French Revolution. Federalists considered the Republican attacks to be illicit and seditious. In 1798, they passed a Sedition Act, authorizing the prosecution of anyone who uttered, printed, or published "any false, scandalous and malicious writing or writings against the government of the United States" with the intent of bringing Congress or the president "into contempt or disrepute."[16]

Republicans responded with another declaration of state-rights constitutionalism. To do it, they relied on the state legislatures of Virginia and Kentucky, which they controlled. The Kentucky and Virginia Resolutions of 1798, written by Jefferson and Madison, respectively, reiterated the principles of state rights and strict construction that Jefferson had articulated in his national bank opinion. Knowing that the Federalist judges who dominated the federal courts would never rule the Sedition Act unconstitutional, the legislatures resolved that each state had the right to evaluate the constitutionality of federal laws and to seek the cooperation of the other states in opposing them. The Federalist-controlled legislatures of other states rejected the Republican constitutional argument. They declared that the United States Supreme Court, not the states, had final authority to assess the constitutionality of federal legislation.

The charge that they were a dangerous and seditious faction forced Republicans to reconsider the legitimacy of parties and the nature of politics. As early as 1792, Madison published essays conceding that, although partisanship remained a vice, party divisions were "natural to most political societies." Jefferson arrived at a similar conclusion. "[I]n every free and deliberating society, there must, from the nature of man, be opposite parties, and violent dissensions and discords," he wrote a political ally in 1798. "Perhaps this party division is necessary to induce each to watch and relate to the people the proceedings of the other."[17]

The congressional and presidential elections of 1800 turned on the constitutional issues that separated Federalist from Republican. For decades afterward, Jeffersonian Republicans and their political descendants, the Democratic Party, would adhere to what they called "the Principles of '98." Jefferson's *Opinion On the Constitutionality of a National Bank* and the Kentucky and Virginia Resolutions would remain the foundational documents of the Democratic Party throughout the nineteenth century.

The result was a sweeping victory for the Republican candidates for president, vice president, and Congress. But the constitutional procedures for electing the president had not accounted for such a party success. The framers had expected the electors to vote for a large number of potential candidates, with the election going over to the House when no one secured a majority. Instead, Federalists and Republicans had nominated a man for each office, and had nominated presidential electors committed only to them. With all the Republican electors casting votes for both Jefferson and their vice-presidential candidate Aaron Burr, the two were tied, and neither had a majority. This left the decision to the lame-duck House of Representatives, where the delegations that would cast votes were evenly divided between Federalists and Republicans. Federalists voted for Burr in order to maintain the deadlock. The impasse continued over six days and thirty-six ballots. In the end, enough Federalists gave way to elect Jefferson.

The crisis of 1800 made clear that the rise of national parties had precipitated a major change in how Americans expected to select their president. Neither Jefferson nor Adams had run on the basis of their character, integrity, and accomplishments—the criteria that the framers had hoped would determine the presidential electors' choice. Each had run as the representative of a party that had articulated a constitutional ideology. Americans had not elected independent presidential electors to choose the best man; they had voted for partisan electors bound to Jefferson or Adams. As far as Republicans were concerned, no technicality arising out of the Constitution's nonpartisan process for selecting a president could justify denying the office to the winner.[18]

Among the first things Americans did after the near disaster of the 1800 elections was to amend the Constitution to change the procedure by which electors chose the president. The Twelfth Amendment to the Constitution separated the vote for vice president from the vote for president, in effect acknowledging that candidates were likely to be nominated on partisan tickets. With parties nominating candidates, it no longer made sense to authorize the House to choose from the top five if none received the vote of a majority in the Electoral College. It would choose from the top three.

In the wake of Jefferson's inauguration in 1801, Americans slowly came to accept the legitimacy and even the necessity of parties. For Federalists, now in the minority, the need to reconsider the legitimacy of partisan opposition was obvious. Despite misgivings, they began to organize effectively for party conflict. Jefferson, in contrast, hoped that well-meaning Federalists would support his administration and that their party would fade away. But whether he fully intended it or not, his conciliatory inaugural address provided perhaps the greatest argument in the American canon for the legitimacy of a "loyal opposition": "[T]hough the will of the majority is in all cases to prevail," he avowed, "the minority possess their equal rights." "[E]very difference of opinion is not a difference of principle." And even where misguided people did reject basic republican principles, let them "stand undisturbed as monument of the safety with which error of opinion may be tolerated where reason is left free to combat it."[19]

Still, antipathy to parties died hard. President James Monroe (1817–1825) envisioned governing through a single, all-encompassing Republican Party. John Quincy Adams would reject the whole notion of party during his presidency (1825–1829). Dismayed Republican purists warned that there would always be a party serving powerful elites who would try to turn government into an engine for their aggrandizement. Preserving the Constitution required constant vigilance on the part of the American people and a permanent party committed to correct constitutional principles. The anti-party Adams went down to defeat in 1828 at the hands of opponents who claimed the Republican Party mantle.

So the first political parties in the United States were organized to contest the meaning of the Constitution. Parties were not yet fully institutionalized, but the pattern had been established. For most of American history, party politics would also be constitutional politics. Parties gave the people the power to decide upon rival understandings of the Constitution by making complicated political issues comprehensible. An analyst who looked at the instances of constitutional rhetoric in Democratic, Whig, and Republican national platforms from 1840 to 2004 has found that references to individual rights appeared in over 90% of them. References to other constitutional issues, such as federalism and the enumeration of governmental powers, constitutional amendments, Supreme Court decisions, judicial powers, and federal enforcement of constitutional rights were found in anywhere from three-quarters to one-third of them. Candidates' acceptance speeches or other key addresses to the public were almost as likely to allude to constitutional issues. The topics remained staples of TV advertising, public polling, and presidential debates.[20]

III. Political Parties and Constitutional Politics

Political parties are essential components of constitutional policy-making in the United States. Throughout American history they have been central to constitutional politics—the process by which the American people interpret and reinterpret the Constitution and apply it in deciding public policy.

Constitutional Politics and Constitutional Law

Since the time they were first organized, parties have presented constitutional issues to the American people. They still do, even though Americans often think of the United States Supreme Court as having the primary responsibility for defining and applying the Constitution.[21] The justices agree. Conceding that disagreements about the meaning of the Constitution's provisions are inevitable, they claim that they alone have the final authority to decide which interpretation is correct.[22] Until recently, law schools have reinforced the common perception and emboldened the judges by teaching generations of lawyers that constitutional questions all resolve into matters of constitutional law decided by judges.

However, the reality is that judges rarely have challenged substantial constitutional decisions made by the American people through the political process. Although judges and lawyers have distinguished law from politics, it is difficult to separate the two in constitutional policy making. The fundamental understandings about the Constitution have come from the American people. The practice of the judges has been to articulate these understandings in the form of constitutional law and to apply them to specific cases fairly and impartially.

Because the United States has a common-law legal system, court decisions on constitutional issues have the authority of precedent. This can lead to problems when the American people reverse their prior understandings of the Constitution. Judges consider themselves bound by precedent, and they tend to value stability in the law. They also tend to see law as separate from politics and are very reluctant to concede that political changes can change the law itself.[23]

This problem is exacerbated by the fact that the terms of federal judges run for life as long as they meet the standard of "good behavior." Americans usually signal new constitutional understandings by replacing elected officials of the political party that represents older constitutional understandings with those of the party that advocates the new ones. Because their terms run for life, federal judges are the last representatives of the older constitutionalism to be replaced. These factors can lead to collisions between the courts and the political branches of government in eras of constitutional change. These collisions are part of our constitutional history and a persistent aspect of constitutional politics. In the end, judges have accommodated fundamental changes in constitutional policy, even as those changes are constrained to some degree by past judicial precedent.

Partisan Eras and the Constitution

Political scientists and historians have identified different eras of political party competition in the United States. Usually new partisan eras, or "partisan regimes," have been associated with changes in party systems, with new ones ushered in by a major realignment of the relationship between the parties, the groups that supported them, and the locations where they received their greatest support.[24] Partisan eras usually have begun with or culminated in a dominant party's simultaneous control of the presidency, both houses of Congress, and ultimately the Supreme Court as well. In each era the dominant party's majority eroded over time, as shifts began in voting behavior and people began to agitate new issues. Party strength became more equal, with neither controlling all branches of the government, until ultimately a new realignment ushered in a new era. Only the long, slow collapse of the party system established in the era of the Great Depression and New Deal seems to have followed a different course.[25]

In the first partisan era, the rivalry between Federalists and Jeffersonian Republicans made clear that the Founders' Constitution had failed to check the rise of parties. In each succeeding era, Americans continued to disagree about how to deal with different problems that profoundly affected their economic interests and their social and religious beliefs. They divided over issues by region, by class, by race, by ethnic background, and even gender. Few acted solely on the basis of constitutional principles. But because Americans take constitutional principles seriously, in each era the divisions have been linked to those principles, with each side claiming the mantle of the Constitution.

Constitutional Politics and the Institutionalization of Parties in the Jacksonian Era

The Democratic Party organized in response to what its founders considered Federalist infiltration of the Jeffersonian Republican Party in the 1810s and 1820s. Promoting an "Era of Good Feeling," Presidents James Monroe and John Quincy Adams had questioned the value of party competition. They had opened the Republican Party to all. Purists charged that Republican leaders were carrying out what seemed to be Federalist policies calling on the federal government to exercise broad constitutional powers. Equally worrying, the Supreme Court, led by Federalist Chief Justice John Marshall, sustained this broad interpretation of federal power, exalted national sovereignty, denied the sovereignty of the states, and vigorously enforced constitutional provisions that limited their powers. Dissidents determined to preserve the "Principles of '98" by reconstituting the Jeffersonian party. Ultimately, they rallied to the presidential candidacy of Andrew Jackson, joining a coalition of political forces that consolidated as the Democratic Party. Jackson defeated incumbent Adams in 1828.[26]

Parties had not fully organized when Jackson ousted Adams, nor did all who backed Jackson understand his position on the issues. He faced a Congress that did not share his constitutional convictions. It is possible he still had not fully formed them. But he soon did. He articulated state-rights, small-government principles in thundering vetoes of nationalistic legislation. Proponents of national action to promote economic development blasted back, but Jackson and his allies gained the upper hand by 1834 and routed their opponents in the presidential and congressional elections of 1836. The Jacksonian party system was founded on constitutional politics, and as a recent analyst has reported, the relationship "between party and the constitutional order increasingly became the preoccupation of politicians on all sides."[27]

Jackson's state-rights-oriented Democrats killed the national bank. They shrank the protective elements of the tariff until they were eliminated in the 1840s. They ended the federal government's direct support of new roads and canals, instead turning money and land over to the states to do the job. They backed states as they flouted national treaties with Native Americans. As seats opened, they confirmed new Supreme Court justices who moderated the nationalistic constitutional doctrines of their predecessors.

The Democratic Party organized at a time when more and more American men were becoming politically active. States entering the Union after 1800 eschewed property restrictions on voting. Older states were in the process of eliminating them, and the new Jacksonian party backed the change vigorously, although in most states they deprived African American men of the vote in the process. Unlike the Federalists and the Jeffersonian Republicans, who relied on elite leaders and appealed to a relatively small number of voters, the Jacksonian Democratic Party was a mass-based political party, as would be the party that organized to oppose it. Both developed local institutions that fostered broad participation of party activists and campaign techniques appealing to a mass electorate.

The Democratic Party's constitutional philosophy encompassed more than state rights. Jackson was convinced that active government always served the interests of the rich and powerful rather than the general welfare. Jacksonians were ostentatiously democratic and hostile to aristocratic pretensions. They not only opposed proposals for state support of economic development, they also opposed state efforts to impose Protestant morality on immigrant groups, especially Irish, German, and French-Canadian Catholics. Commitment to what Democrats called "personal liberty" became another key tenet of the Democratic Party.

The Jacksonians saw theirs as the party of the Constitution. The first plank of the party's platform resolved "[t]hat the Federal Government is one of limited powers, derived solely from the Constitution, and the grants of power shown therein ought to be strictly construed by all the departments and agents of the government, and that it is inexpedient and dangerous to exercise doubtful constitutional powers."[28] That remained the first plank of every Democratic platform until 1860. Seeing their party as the bulwark of the Constitution, Democrats did everything they could to strengthen it. They organized local campaign meetings. They subsidized party newspapers, often with government printing contracts. They filled government offices with their partisans. Democrats' opponents soon emulated them.[29] Nonetheless, Jackson's critics charged him with exercising despotic power. They called themselves Whigs, after the opponents of tyrannical British governments. They excoriated Democrats making government a mere tool of their party. On the campaign trail and in Congress, the Whigs often blasted Democrats' crabbed interpretation of federal power. But they were cautious about challenging Democrats' popular state-rights constitutional-ism too directly. On the state level, they were more outspoken in favor of using government power to promote economic development, education, and good morals.[30]

Whigs expressed their nationalist constitutional ideas most vocally when defending the Union from southern extremists like South Carolina's John C. Calhoun Calhoun argued that the states remained sovereign, could nullify unconstitutional federal legislation, and could even secede from the Union. Such threats gave Whig leaders like Daniel Webster the opportunity to articulate their nationalist constitutional philosophy. The states did not create the Union, and they could not destroy it. The federal government posed no threat to liberty; it was its best guarantor. "Liberty and Union, now and for ever, one and inseparable!" Webster thundered.[31]

Jackson too denounced nullification and secession, but from a state-rights standpoint. He was devoted to strict construction of federal power and preservation of state jurisdiction, but when Congress passed a law exceeding its powers, individual states could not nullify it, he warned. The states may have created the Union, but they created a nation when they did so. From then on, no state had the right to secede. This was the version of state rights that the Democratic Party presented to the American people. But when most of the southern nullificationists followed Calhoun into the Democratic Party in the 1840s, they brought their commitment to state sovereignty with them.[32]

Parties and the Constitution in the Civil War and Reconstruction Partisan Era

By the 1840s, the sharp distinction between Democrats and Whigs began to blur. At the same time, the slavery issue began to crowd out the economic issues that had characterized the second party system. Constitutional issues were at the heart of the debate.[33] Most Democratic politicians argued that jurisdiction over slavery lay entirely with the states. They warned that the Union could be preserved only by keeping federal and state jurisdictions strictly separate, leaving the southern states solely responsible for slavery. They charged anyone who agitated the issue with disunionism.

But there were too many places where the federal government *was* involved. Slavery existed in the capital itself, subject entirely to the federal government. The federal government had direct authority over new territories. It had the power to regulate interstate commerce and therefore the slave trade. While northern Democrats urged strict federal government neutrality over slavery, more and more southern Democrats insisted that the federal government was constitutionally obligated to protect slave property like any other. In contrast, opponents of slavery insisted that the federal government exercise its constitutional powers in the interest of freedom.

The second party system could not contain the conflict, and a new one replaced it in the 1850s. The Republican Party replaced the Whigs as the Democrats' main opponents.[34] Republicans insisted that the Constitution was established to carry out the principles of freedom expressed in the Declaration of Independence. Yet the "slave power" had been pressing ever more successfully to pervert the Constitution into a bastion of slavery. As if to confirm the charge, in 1857 the Supreme Court ruled that free African Americans were not citizens of the United States and that Congress had no power to bar slavery from the territories.[35] Republicans repudiated the decision and vowed to restore the Constitution to its original antislavery principles. They got their chance when Democrats divided in 1860 over southern demands, encouraged by the Court's holding, that the government enact a slave code for the territories. When Republican Abraham Lincoln won the presidency over the divided opposition, the southern states exercised what most southerners claimed was their constitutional right to secede from the Union.* Northern Democrats joined Republicans in denouncing secession and supporting war if necessary to restore the Union.

Republicans dominated the third party era. Local economic interests and ethnic and religious background played a key role in determining partisan allegiance, but the issues were once again articulated in constitutional terms. During the Civil War and the period of Reconstruction that followed it, Republicans stressed national sovereignty and power. They tied their party to patriotism and nationalist constitutionalism. During the Reconstruction period, from 1865 to the mid-1870s, they exercised federal power to an unprecedented degree to restore the Union, to reconstruct southern state governments on the basis of freedom and equality, and to protect citizens' civil and political rights. Republicans underwrote the expansion of transportation and communications, created a system of national banks, reestablished a protective tariff, subsidized education, encouraged the settlement of western lands, and fostered a national market as free as possible from restrictions imposed by state governments.[36]

Democrats continued to press for strict construction of federal power and to defend local autonomy. They decried Lincoln's broad claims of presidential power. They blasted abuse of the war powers to inaugurate a military draft and to confiscate property. They denied federal power to impose political and social changes in the South as part of the reconstruction of the Union. They fought desperately to prevent the addition of the Thirteenth, Fourteenth, and Fifteenth Amendments, which wrote Republican constitutional doctrines into the Constitution itself. The amendments abolished slavery, guaranteed equal rights and due process to all, forbade racial discrimination in voting, and—worst, from Democrats' perspective—authorized Congress to pass "appropriate" legislation to enforce the provisions. "If sanctioned by the people," they declared in

---

* Some southerners, especially former Whigs, defended secession as a right of revolution rather than a constitutional right. And a significant number opposed secession itself but loyally supported their states once the decision to secede was made.

their 1868 national platform, Republican policies "can only end in a single centralized and consolidated government, in which the separate existence of the States will be entirely absorbed, and an unqualified despotism be established in place of a federal union of co-equal States."[37] Defeated on the issue, Democrats grudgingly conceded that the Fourteenth and Fifteenth Amendments had become a part of the Constitution, but they did their best to interpret them to protect state rights and minimize federal power. Even Republicans became concerned that the pendulum had swung too far toward centralization, and congressional power to enforce the amendments was narrowly construed in the last decades of the nineteenth century, to the great damage of African Americans.[38]

Republicans maintained control of all three branches of the government from 1861 to 1875. During that time parties became more completely dominant in the political system than they ever would be again. A powerful patronage system, bitterly partisan newspapers, highly organized and localized campaign organizations, and political positions polarized largely on constitutional issues turned the parties into rival political armies. Voter turnout reached the highest levels they ever have in American history, and so did party regularity in voting. Rarely was there much difference in the vote received by the strongest party candidate and the weakest.[39]

The Republican Party's dominance gradually eroded after 1875, as Americans turned from Civil War issues to new ones raised by the transition from an agricultural to an industrial economy. Many Americans demanded that government at all levels of the federal system take action to protect workers, farmers, and small businessmen against the growing power of monopolistic corporations and their financial allies. Dissatisfied with Democrats' and Republicans' floundering efforts, they turned to a third party—the People's Party, or "Populists." The Populists took a broad view of federal authority. They called for sweeping action to counteract growing corporate power; national ownership of railroads, the telegraph, and the telephone; and a graduated income tax.[40]

As Republicans and Democrats tried to cope, constitutional rhetoric played a smaller role, but their rival constitutional ideas continued to affect their approaches. Both parties backed federal action to regulate railroad rates and regulations, but over Democratic opposition Republicans supported (and secured) a more centralized program with a new national Interstate Commerce Commission to superintend the whole subject. Republicans proposed to outlaw all business monopolies that affected interstate commerce. Democrats insisted that the federal government could outlaw only those monopolies that directly engaged in interstate commerce. Most of all, Republicans insisted that the protective tariff was necessary to protect American workers from low-waged, foreign competition; Democrats continued to call it unconstitutional.[41]

The federal courts took a stronger role in resolving constitutional issues than they had in the first two party systems, generally reflecting the constitutional ideology of the Republican Party that appointed most of the justices. The courts' first concern was to protect the national market against local controls. As the third party system decayed and Populists gained strength, judges also began to intervene to maintain what they saw as basic constitutional principles. When newly established state commissions regulated various aspects of transportation, the Supreme Court held that due process required judicial review of the rules to preclude arbitrary deprivations of property. The Court held that the Constitution protected "liberty of contract." Only exceptional circumstances justified government interference. On this basis the courts reviewed and sometimes overturned laws protecting workers from exploitation. When Democrats and Populists in Congress passed a tax on the income of wealthier Americans, the Supreme Court ruled it unconstitutional. The justices frustrated Congress's efforts to counteract monopolies, barring the application of its antitrust law to farms, mines, and industrial production, which the justices said lay within state rather than federal jurisdiction. The decisions encouraged constitutional challenges to all sorts of laws affecting business interests, and lower federal courts regularly cited Supreme Court precedents to find reform measures unconstitutional. In these decisions, the Supreme Court entrenched in law the policies and underlying constitutional philosophy that characterized the third party system, undercutting the legitimacy of the reforms advocated by the Populists and the growing number of reformers in the Democratic and Republican Parties.[42]

Parties and the Constitution in the Progressive Era Party System

A new, fourth party system emerged out of all these conflicts around the turn of the twentieth century. During the so-called Progressive Era, the Republican Party reclaimed political dominance, but both parties responded to the Progressive ideas that captivated Americans. All sorts of reforms were associated with Progressivism. They were varied and sometimes contradictory, and often drew support from different groups. But what Progressives had in common was a belief that the government was the best instrument with which to confront social and economic problems.

Both parties advocated state and federal action to deal with the problems of industrialization. Republican President Theodore Roosevelt used his powers to promote the public interest against what he saw as abuses of corporate power. Under his more conservative successor William Howard Taft, Republicans took credit for exercising federal power to promote economic prosperity and stability while balancing the interests of businessmen, workers, farmers, and consumers. Democrats minimized their traditional appeals to state rights and stressed instead their tradition of opposition to special privileges for the rich and powerful. They abandoned their commitment to strict construction of federal power. In their 1912 platform Democrats urged "the full exercise of all the powers of Government, both State and national." They declared that it was "as necessary that the Federal government shall exercise the powers delegated to it as that the States shall exercise the powers reserved to them."[43]

In 1912 Roosevelt bolted the Republican Party and demanded even more far-reaching federal laws to combat corporate control of the economy and further action to reform the political process. His Progressive Party platform proposed "bringing under effective national jurisdiction those problems which have expanded beyond reach of the individual states," both by broad interpretation of the federal government's constitutional powers and, where necessary, by constitutional amendment. It denounced the doctrine of state rights as an obstacle to administering "the affairs of a union of States which have in all essential respects become one people."[44]

The Progressives knew that they were engaging in constitutional politics. "We hold . . . that the people are the masters of their Constitution," they declared. It was the people's responsibility to "fulfill its purposes and to safeguard it from those who, by perversion of its intent, would convert it into an instrument of injustice." The admonition was aimed not only at conservative Republicans and Democrats but at federal and state judges and the Supreme Court. Another plank called for "such restriction of the power of the courts as shall leave to the people the ultimate authority to determine fundamental questions of social welfare and public policy."[45]

Roosevelt failed to secure the presidency in 1912, dividing the Republican vote and losing to Democrat Woodrow Wilson. Despite his party's state-rights heritage, Wilson won congressional approval for a wide range of progressive federal legislation. When Democrats renominated him in 1916, their platform failed to mention the Constitution for the first time in the party's history. Instead it took credit for a number of federal programs and promised more. In 1920 it was the Republican platform, rather than the Democrats', that contained a section entitled "Constitutional Government." It denounced "executive autocracy" and promised to adhere to a federal system in which the state and federal governments "each act within its constitutional powers."[46]

The Supreme Court accommodated the shift toward more active state and federal government. Without explicitly overruling the precedents it had set in the 1890s and early 1900s, it upheld state laws regulating the workplace, expanded its conception of interstate commerce, and sustained the broad uses of state and federal power during the war. Only as the fourth party system went into decline after World War One did the courts begin to challenge the expansion of government activity that characterized the Progressive Era.[47]

Parties and the Constitution in the New Deal Party System

As the fourth party system eroded, both parties split into progressive and conservative wings on economic issues. Likewise they split on the question of personal liberty versus the power of government to enforce the majority's moral values. The Ku Klux Klan, dedicated to preserving conservative Protestant cultural and political supremacy against foreign, Jewish, Catholic, and African American influences, was strong in both political parties. The Klan's opponents, combining a belief in active government with a commitment to toleration, identified themselves as liberals. In 1924 Klan-backed conservatives fought more liberal Democrats for 103 ballots before the party could nominate a compromise candidate. The Klan objected particularly to the nomination of the front-runner, the anti-prohibition, Catholic governor of New York, Al Smith. By 1928 the Democrats' shift toward tolerance was evident: Smith won on the first ballot.[48]

The Great Depression of 1929, which lasted a decade, disrupted the decaying fourth party system and brought in a new one. Once again constitutional issues were central. When the Republican Party failed to prevent widespread suffering as the economy collapsed, Americans turned to the Democrats. President Franklin Delano Roosevelt, elected in 1932, completed the Democratic Party's transformation from the party of state rights and small government to the party of broad construction of federal power and active government at every level. He tied this change to the Democrats' traditional hostility toward special privileges. Given the changes in America's industrial society, it was no longer possible to eliminate special privileges by keeping government out of the economy. Only government could guarantee an equal chance to all. "Our government . . . owes to every one an avenue to possess himself of a portion of that plenty sufficient for his needs through his own work," he said.[49] In office, he promised a "New Deal" for the American people.

Taking office at the depths of the Depression, Roosevelt took radical action. To prevent the imminent collapse of the financial system, he declared a "bank holiday," reopening only those banks formally found to be sound. He took the country off the gold standard. Congress complemented such unilateral exercises of executive power by passing a series of hastily (and clumsily) drawn statutes authorizing the president to set up administrative agencies through which representatives of various industries, organized labor, and the public set up "codes of conduct" to govern production, marketing, wages, hours, and other employment practices. It did the same for agriculture. The federal government used its spending power to begin construction of massive dams to control floods and supply electric power to regions that had been slow to develop. These programs provided jobs, but the government went further, employing huge numbers of Americans in a wide variety of public works projects administered by new federal agencies created for the purpose.

The conservative wing of the Republican Party challenged the constitutionality of many of these programs. They exceeded the power delegated to the federal government and interfered with property rights and liberty of contract, conservatives argued. Their opposition grew as Democrats created Social Security, a pension system for most American workers, and followed this with a law to foster the organization of labor unions across American industry. State governments passed parallel legislation regulating business and agriculture and setting minimum standards of employment and wages.[50]

The Supreme Court added its influence to the voices challenging the constitutionality of such government actions. They took a hard line against the constitutionality of state laws protecting workers and federal New Deal legislation in general. Bound by the decisions of the Supreme Court, local federal judges were bringing much of the New Deal to a standstill as Americans went to the polls in 1936.[51]

The presidential and congressional elections of 1936 were a great referendum on the New Deal's expansion of federal authority and presidential power. The Democratic platform listed program after program that promoted recovery and blasted Republicans for "propos[ing] to meet many pressing national problems solely by action of the separate States." "[D]rought, dust storms, floods, minimum wages, maximum hours, child labor, and working conditions in industry, monopolistic and unfair business practices cannot be adequately handled exclusively by 48 separate State legislatures, 48 separate State administrations and 48 separate State courts."[52]

The Republican platform blasted the New Deal. Nearly all of the objections were constitutional. "The powers of Congress have been usurped by the President," the list of charges began. "The integrity and authority of the Supreme Court have been flouted. The rights and liberties of American citizens have been violated. Regulated monopoly has displaced free enterprise. The New Deal Administration constantly seeks to usurp the rights reserved to the States and to the people. It has insisted on the passage of laws contrary to the Constitution."[53] The fifth party system completed the remarkable reversal of the Democratic and Republican Parties on constitutional issues.

The resounding Democratic victory in 1936 marked the triumph of liberal constitutionalism—a combination of broad construction of federal power and a commitment to tolerance and individual liberty. It cemented a political coalition of organized labor, city-dwellers, and the targets of extreme proponents of white Protestant supremacy—Catholics, Jews, and African Americans—augmented by a still solidly Democratic South.

Despite this mandate, Roosevelt worried that the Supreme Court might rule the rest of the New Deal legislative program unconstitutional before he had a chance to nominate new justices. To counteract the danger, he proposed increasing their number. He lambasted the justices for confusing their personal and political beliefs with the mandates of the Constitution. "We have . . . reached the point as a Nation where we must take action to save the Constitution from the Court," he urged. Americans wanted "a Supreme Court that will . . . refuse to amend the Constitution by the arbitrary exercise of judicial power."[54]

Roosevelt need not have worried. Considering laws that were better written and sustained by stronger constitutional arguments, and probably sobered by the results of the election, a new majority of the justices sustained New Deal laws and state regulations of the economy and workplace. As a result, Roosevelt's court-packing initiative collapsed. Nonetheless, it would be forty years before the Supreme Court would again rule a federal law unconstitutional on state-rights grounds. The justices sustained the constitutionality of broad delegations of legislative and adjudicative power to executive agencies, as long as the law provided for final recourse to the federal courts.[55]

For four decades, the New Deal idea that the federal government had nearly unlimited power to regulate and promote the national economy went virtually unchallenged. The principle expanded into such areas as public health, education, environmental regulation, and protection of the civil and political rights of minority groups and women. Democrats no longer considered the Constitution to be primarily a restraint on government. It was "a charter of individual freedom," but it was also "an effective instrument for human progress," the party's platform declared in 1952. Instead of stressing state rights as a bulwark against invasive federal government, the platform praised federal programs for relying on states for their administration—"fine examples," it observed, "of Federal-State cooperation." Presidents continued to exercise the expansive powers Roosevelt bequeathed them and remained the focal point of American politics and policy making thereafter. They became the main expositors of party programs and ideologies. The party that does not hold the presidency has had more difficulty in making its positions clear and coherent, although in recent decades congressional leaders have played an important part in articulating Republican philosophy.[56]

The end of World War Two began a long period of decline and decay of the fifth party system. Partisan loyalties weakened, the Democratic Party lost simultaneous control of the presidency and Congress, and new issues began to challenge the economic ones on which the New Deal party system had been based. Democrats and Republicans disagreed over how to balance national security concerns with freedom of political expression and association. But overall, differences between the parties over political and constitutional issues shrank. When political scientists for the first time systematically analyzed ordinary citizens' political beliefs, they were shocked at how little ideological consistency they found and how little substantial knowledge of the Constitution, despite abstract veneration.[57]

Some changes associated with the decay of a party system appeared to become permanent. Politicians became more and more independent of party organizations. They established their own campaign committees, raised their own money for elections, and broke with their parties' political positions more and more often. Presidential candidates set up campaign committees whose operations dwarfed those of the parties in whose name they ran. Campaign contributions from special and public-interest groups became the fuel of politics, and their lobbyists became more important in developing public policy than more general and abstract public opinion. Newspapers had become nonpartisan, no longer shaping the news to encourage party loyalty nor transmitting the party line to readers. Primary elections reduced the influence of party leaders. In the case of presidential primaries, the winner was often decided before the parties' national conventions even met.

In such an environment, fewer and fewer voters identified strongly with a political party or could identify its positions clearly and accurately. More and more they split votes among candidates of different parties running for different offices. By the 1970s analysts identified an era of "dealignment" rather than realignment. The party system seemed to have changed fundamentally but not in the traditional way. It appeared to be a party era without parties. Analysts wondered if political parties any longer fulfilled a significant role in the creation of public policy. Instead, they suggested, the parties' primary constitutional role was to legitimate the political process.[58]

Parties and Constitutional Politics in the Civil Rights Era

Although there was no sudden and dramatic partisan realignment among voters as in prior transitions to new partisan eras, a strong pro-Democratic tide in the congressional elections of 1958 led to Democratic control of the presidency and Congress from 1960 to 1968, with Democrats making up a majority of Supreme Court justices as well.[59] The consequence was a wave of legislation that radically extended the power of the federal government to define and protect the civil and political rights of African Americans, ethnic and religious minorities, and women. At the same time the Democrats enacted New Deal-like legislation to provide health care for older Americans and a general "war on poverty." Finally, as a new generation of Americans demanded unprecedented personal freedom from traditional social constraints on personal behavior, the Constitution was reinterpreted to guarantee broad rights of privacy and personal choice.

In contrast to prior partisan eras, the parties did not polarize around these issues. By 1948 both parties' national platforms endorsed civil-rights legislation, leading many southern Democrats to organize a bolting States' Rights Democratic Party. Liberals in both parties offered constitutional justifications for federal promotion of civil liberty, equal rights, and economic security, while conservatives in both denounced them. In 1964, the conservatives briefly gained control of the Republican Party. They nominated the party's most vocal critic of the era's legislation for president on a platform denouncing "Federal extremists—impulsive in the use of national power." It charged that "freedom, diversity and individual, local and state responsibility have given way to regimentation, conformity and subservience to central power."[60] The result was an overwhelming repudiation of the conservative critique. When Democrats did lose control of the presidency in 1968, Republican President Richard Nixon continued and even expanded many federal programs, and endorsed new initiatives to preserve the environment.

The Supreme Court played a more prominent role in making constitutional policy during the Civil Rights era than it ever had before. Instead of instituting a holding action, as it had in past transitions, it took the lead in promoting constitutional change. Like the political parties, the justices were no longer concerned with the boundary between state and federal authority. Instead they began to concentrate on constitutional issues that many Americans doubted could be resolved fairly by the democratic process—issues involving the relationship between government, individual rights, and the rights of minority groups. The Court's landmark ruling against state-enforced school segregation in *Brown v. Board of Education*[61] was the emblem of the new era.

From the 1940s onward, state and federal judges reinterpreted the Bill of Rights and the Fourteenth Amendment to impose ever stricter limits on the power of government to impinge on civil liberty and equal—banning prayer and religious education in schools, expanding freedom of speech and the press, overturning laws against contraception and abortion, and expanding the rights of those accused of crime. As a consequence, the foremost constitutional issues of the time were reconceived to be matters of constitutional law rather than constitutional politics. Observers wrote of "the judicialization of politics." While extreme conservatives denounced the Court for an unconstitutional usurpation of power, most Americans came to see the Supreme Court rather than political majorities as having the final responsibility for carrying out constitutional mandates. The Supreme Court's articulation of constitutional law replaced popular constitutionalism as the main determinant of constitutional policy[62]

This expansion of judicial power raised a difficult question. In a democracy, how could one reconcile giving final authority in such controversial areas to judges? As constitutional philosophers struggled with this "counter-majoritarian difficulty," those who disagreed with the Supreme Court's decisions attacked them as essentially political rather than legal.[63] When support for the programs associated with the Civil Rights era waned, this disagreement became a crucial element in the establishment of a new partisan era.

Constitutional Politics in the Conservative Partisan Era

Support for the liberal constitutionalism of the Civil Rights era began to wane in the late 1960s, as more and more people reacted against the Supreme Court-led assault on government imposition of traditional social values President Nixon worked to harness this resentment. In a major political realignment, white southerners began to abandon the Democratic Party for the Republicans, leading to a South as solidly Republican in presidential elections as it had been Democratic earlier. Slowly but surely, the political revolution extended to southern congressional and state elections as well. By 2015 all but one U.S. senator from the South* was a Republican. Republicans had gained control of the state legislatures of every southern state but Kentucky. The realignment in the North was less dramatic but equally significant. The Republican Party's opposition to liberal legislation and court decisions challenging traditional values led to a shift toward the Republican Party among white evangelical Protestants and conservative Catholics. Republicans and Democrats came to differ more

---

* By the South, I mean the Confederate states plus Kentucky.

and more radically on what the Constitution required when it came to social issues like remedies for past racial discrimination, abortion, prayer in the schools, pornography, and gay rights.[64]

In the 1970s workers' earnings stagnated and the economy became unstable. Many Americans turned against federal programs to fight poverty and the taxes necessary to pay for them. To some degree, Republicans succeeded in linking the tax issue to racial resentments, charging that tax revenues went to an undeserving, disproportionately African American class of welfare recipients. This attack directly challenged the constitutional underpinnings of the New Deal general-welfare state.[65] In 1980, the Republican Party exploited these issues to elect President Ronald Reagan, the most conservative chief executive since before the New Deal. Although Republicans would not gain control of all branches of the federal government until the turn of the twenty-first century, they secured control of Congress and the Supreme Court by the mid-1990s. Presidential elections generally remained closely contested, but the geographic sources of the parties' support had substantially changed. Party lines tightened dramatically, and parties once again polarized on the issues.[66]

Republicans made conservative constitutionalism a central element of their political ideology. "We seek to restore the family, the neighborhood, the community, and the workplace as vital alternatives in our national life to ever-expanding federal power," they proclaimed in their 1980 national platform. In his inaugural address, Reagan expressed the Republican position simply and clearly: "[G]overnment is not the solution to our problem; government is the problem."[67] Administration officials, conservative commentators, judges, and law professors demanded that the Supreme Court exercise "judicial restraint" when considering the constitutionality of political decisions. The justices should adhere to the "original understanding" of constitutional language when it was framed and ratified rather than reinterpret it to conform to liberal ideas of individual liberty and equal rights. As usual, the justices reflected the dominant view that had been established through the political system. Although observers were surprised by occasional manifestations of liberalism, the justices more often cut back on the rulings of the Civil Rights era. As Republicans gained firmer control of the government, the Court became more aggressive in ruling liberal programs unconstitutional.[68]

The Democratic Party continued to advocate federal protection of civil liberty, equal rights, and the environment, but it quickly gave way on federal regulation of business and financial institutions, federal poverty-fighting programs, and raising the taxes necessary to pay for federal programs. When Republicans advocated using government to promote conservative "family values," Democrats insisted that such programs violated constitutional protections of personal liberty. Republicans urged that government programs take account of religious influence in American society. Democrats called such programs unconstitutional violations of the First Amendment's mandate for separation of church and state.

The election of a Democratic Congress in 2006 and a Democratic president in 2008 seemed to challenge the dominance of conservativism that had characterized the conservative partisan era. President Barack Obama and the Democratic Congress created a new federal health insurance program that rivaled Social Security and Medicare in its bold use of federal power to solve economic problems. But rather than marking the emergence of a new political era, the program elicited a powerful reaction that showed that the issues that characterized the latest party era remained firmly in place. Moreover, the debate over the issues became more intensely constitutional in character, with a vocal and influential wing of the Republican Party demanding a return to what its members claimed to be original constitutional principles of limited government and state rights.[69] President Obama interpreted his power to issue executive orders broadly to overcome trenchant Republican resistance to his programs. Republicans denounced his actions as unconstitutional instances of executive tyranny. The most ideological of Republican conservatives called themselves the Tea Party, alluding to radicals who challenged overreaching central authority in the run up to the Revolution. But all Republicans shared their commitment to constitutional government as they interpreted it. "We are the party of the Constitution," the party platform declared in 2012, in contrast "to the antipathy toward the Constitution" they attributed to Democrats.[70]

Democrats, in contrast, consistently urged active government to remedy a variety of problems, without articulating a constitutional philosophy to sustain it. For them, the Constitution was relevant primarily in its protection of equal rights and liberties.[71] With President Obama winning reelection in 2012 but Republicans regaining control of Congress in 2014, party lines appeared more starkly drawn than at any time since the Civil War/Reconstruction party era.

Americans no longer rely on the parties for most of their political information, but they remain a key part of the process. Although politicians are more independent of parties than they have been in the past, parties once again have become the key conduit through which voters' constitutional choices are applied to public policy.

It is less clear whether the revival of popular constitutionalism portends a shift away from the Supreme Court as the primary determinant of constitutional policy through the justices' articulation of constitutional law.

Certainly justices are affected by shifts in public opinion, but they remain committed to the ideas that law is separate from politics, that it is their job to declare what the law of the Constitution is, and that, in the end, that determination must prevail. Americans still have not resolved the degree to which the rule of law must mean the rule of judges.

IV. OTHER CONSTITUTIONAL
FUNCTIONS OF POLITICAL PARTIES

Some analysts have perceived a tension between political parties and the Constitution dating back to the Founders' original hostility to them. From this perspective, parties provide extra-constitutional means for enacting public policy, substituting popular will for the elitist government the Constitution tried to establish.[72] However, it is more accurate to see parties as an important part of a constitutional system that consists of far more than the written Constitution itself.

Forging Governing Majorities

Having fought the Revolutionary War to resist British tyranny, the Founders were more concerned with liberty than anything else. They framed the Constitution to replace a weak confederation of states with a new federal union characterized by strong central government. This decision raised the problem of how to keep the government from being so strong that it could deprive the people of their rights. As explained above, the framers' answer was to prevent the concentration of power through the system of "separation of powers" and "checks and balances." But they had broken up government so completely that nothing might get done at all. The Constitution could have been a prescription for deadlock and paralysis.

When Federalists united to carry out Hamilton's proposals during what analysts call the first party system, it became clear that one of the main functions of political parties would be to overcome this danger. As future president Woodrow Wilson explained in a seminal analysis of constitutional government in America, the government's operations "can be solidified and drawn into a system only by the external authority of party." Parties "are absolutely necessary to hold . . . things . . . together and give some coherence to the action of political forces."[73]

Party ties have by no means led public officials to act as one over American history. Policy making under the American constitutional system is too fragmented for that. There has always been dissension, but party ideologies have been strong enough to bind like-minded politicians on the great issues that have divided Americans over the course of their history.[74] In the nineteenth century, especially, the parties stressed those issues that united them and minimized those that divided them. In the Jacksonian era, for example, both Democrats and Whigs stressed economic issues and tried to suppress those involving slavery. When Democrats and Whigs no longer could keep the slavery issue out of politics, the Jacksonian-era party system collapsed, and both the leaders and the adherents of the two parties divided. The same was true of the party system that followed. The new Republican Party stressed issues arising out of the Civil War for as long as they could. After that they united on the protective tariff. Maintaining unity on those issues, Republicans were able to carry out their policies despite the fragmented nature of American government. Because East, West, and South had different economic and financial interests, those issues threatened the unity of both parties. When they no longer could suppress them, the third party system disintegrated.

In the twentieth century, parties became even more diverse than they had been in the nineteenth. Parties had to broker agreements among various interests to get things done. As ties between politicians and their parties eroded after the 1960s, parties became less and less effective in forging majorities. But the party system that developed in the late twentieth century has been characterized by party divisions more like those of the past. Parties have become more ideologically homogenous and more closely identified with different special interests. With the parties equally balanced, united, and in control of different branches of the government, the result has been partisan deadlock. Scholarly observers wonder whether the nation has become ungovernable.[75] But history suggests that one party or the other will win the support of the American people and then be able to establish its program, fulfilling parties' traditional role in the constitutional system.

Recruitment of Public Servants

The Constitution gives the president the responsibility for nominating important executive officers, as defined by Congress, requiring him to send their names to the Senate for confirmation. Presidents turned to the heads of government departments—the members of their cabinets—for names. They in turn relied on local political allies to suggest potential nominees. After 1820 the terms of most federal appointees ran for four years, but until Andrew Jackson became president, capable officials had generally been reappointed.

Jackson's supporters made the process much more political.[76] The new president removed federal officers who opposed his party, replacing them with political supporters. Jackson justified his actions by stressing the value of "rotation" in office. Otherwise, government would be run by an elite of permanent officers, unresponsive to public opinion, and appointed through their connections with the elite leaders he had just displaced. His principle of "rotation" opened government jobs to ordinary Americans, suggested by local party leaders. They were expected to support their patrons—hence, the term "patronage" to describe the relationship.

With the presidents nominating and the Senate confirming the appointment of postmasters in every town and hamlet in the country, the connection between local politicians and their Washington allies was strong. Pension agents were equally important to the local communities they served. They administered the government's programs to support disabled veterans, the wives and children of those who had fallen in battle, and eventually the survivors of anyone who had served in the nation's armed forces. Well-paid, prestigious positions in the diplomatic corps, the Department of the Treasury, and the Department of the Interior went to influential politicians and community leaders. Whigs criticized the "spoils system," but they followed the same practices when they gained control of the White House.

During the third party system, the dominant Republican Party tied appointments even more closely to party organization.[77] United States senators became the main conduits through which local party leaders recommended appointments to the president. For a time, senators could keep appointees in office by refusing to confirm successors, making appointees even more dependent upon their goodwill. Senators became the most powerful figures—the "bosses"—in their states' parties. Other leaders often felt slighted, and governors would often name state-government employees who were on the outs with federal appointees. Things could get even worse if both U.S. senators were from the same party and a rivalry developed between them. Where his party did not hold a Senate seat, the president and the department heads relied on advice from other party leaders, stoking yet more jealousies. Unhappy with this unseemly factionalism and boss-control, many Americans began to call for reform to take the politics out of the civil service.

In the 1870s, department heads began to develop examinations, beginning the slow process by which merit would replace political connection as the main criterion for appointment. In 1883 Congress passed a Civil Service Act that authorized the president to classify government positions as nonpolitical, with terms to last as long as their occupants fulfilled their responsibilities. Over time, presidents brought more and more positions under this protected status. At the turn of the twentieth century, there were still 100,000 positions within the patronage system.

By the century's end, only a few thousand remained, out of a total workforce of nearly three million. At the same time, rules prohibiting federal employees from playing active roles in political parties grew stricter, culminating in the Hatch Act of 1939, which barred all but a few federal employees from participating in partisan political activity.[78] In 1990, the Supreme Court turned constitutional policy into constitutional law, holding that the First Amendment barred discrimination in government employment based on political affiliation.[79] Parties no longer fulfill a significant role in recruiting government workers, but despite the Supreme Court's decision, party leaders manage to help and reward friends when they can.[80]

Opening Government Positions to Ordinary Citizens

The framers hoped that the political system established by the Constitution would serve as a "filter"—promoting the election of the most worthy, able, educated, and honest class of men to Congress and the presidency. They deprecated an aristocracy of birth, but they were committed to an aristocracy of talent rewarded by wealth, social status, and influence. Presidents Washington, Adams, Jefferson, and Madison, their cabinets, and the members of Congress all belonged to an American upper class. If parties had not developed, the Constitution would have led to government by an elite.

This changed with the rise of Andrew Jackson and the establishment of the second party system.[81] Parties developed mass support. Voters more and more voted for a party and its principles rather than for a man and his character. Parties printed "tickets" listing the names of their candidates. These were deposited directly into the ballot box. If one wanted to vote for someone else, he had to "scratch" the name of his party's candidate and write in the name of the competitor.

The skills required by party politics differed from those required of planters, merchants, and members of the educated professions. Parties held local, district, and state conventions, and political rallies open to all white men. Rich candidates had once courted voters by supplying food and drink at political rallies. Now the parties organized the rallies and supplied the food, the drink, and the speakers. Where elite candidates once commanded respect, party politicians relied on the "common touch."

Parties relied on active workers to win elections. They had to organize the conventions and rallies, circulate documents, and influence voters. If they received a government position as a reward, they were expected to contribute money to the party coffers. All too often they engaged in various forms of corruption to raise money that was kicked back to their party organizations. Nominees for elective office also were chosen not only for their general ability and popularity but for their party services. They were expected to have campaigned for party candidates, spoken at party rallies, contributed to campaign war chests. In sum, the rise of parties led to the rise of professional politicians, who made their living from the offices to which they were appointed or elected. Any man with talent and dedication could gain economic security and social prominence through politics. Politics became one of the most important avenues to social advancement.[82]

Making Issues Comprehensible to the Public

The framers had not much liked the popular politics that had been developing in the states during the Revolution and immediately afterward. They believed that the people could be trusted to protect their liberties. Actual government, however, was something else. That should be left to wise and educated leaders elected by a virtuous but deferential population. But when the Founders themselves divided over public policy in the 1790s, each side saw itself as defending constitutional liberty and appealed to the public for support. The contestants were compelled to explain the issues, and they did it by publishing letters, pamphlets, and formal public documents, organizing parades and rallies, establishing political clubs, circulating newspapers, issuing broadsides and putting up posters. By the Jacksonian and Civil War/Reconstruction eras, parties augmented such efforts with political conventions and formal political platforms, the circulation of speeches made in Congress, and "stump" speeches delivered at campaign rallies, all covered copiously by newspapers that sympathized with one party or the other and received various kinds of financial support.

The purpose of all this was to make issues comprehensible to the general public. Congressional speeches and weighty pamphlet publications were aimed at the educated, whether publicly or self-taught. But stump speeches and newspaper editorials put the issues into words ordinary voters could understand. Partisan and nonpartisan political manuals and handbooks published political platforms, excerpts from congressional and stump speeches, public letters, and compilations of information. Banners at rallies and parades, broadsides, posters, and campaign songs distilled the party's message into a few, pithy words. Cartoons made issues clear in emotionally packed illustrations, sometimes crude, sometimes sophisticated.[83]

In the twentieth century, other sources augmented and then replaced the political parties as the main source of political information. Independent journals of opinion proliferated in the 1890s and after. Newspapers became independent of the parties. Radio and television stations rarely had partisan affiliations. Universities, think tanks, public interest groups, special interest groups, and public intellectuals all became alternative sources of information. Punchy radio and television ads more and more replaced campaign literature and speeches. Parties' efforts to present coherent public platforms were drowned out. The clamor of alternative voices made it more difficult for ordinary voters to form comprehensive political ideologies. By midcentury voters seemed awash in conflicting ideas that most could not place in a general context.[84]

This changed in the following decades. Beginning in the late 1970s, political parties, especially the Republican Party, became more ideologically uniform and more representative of particular economic interests and religious values. The advent of cable television and new electronic media fostered the rise of liberal and conservative cable news channels. There was a growing tendency to secure political information from television, radio, and online political commentators rather than traditional newspapers and television news programs that valued objectivity and nonpartisanship. As a result, sources of information and opinion began to coincide with party positions rather than crosscut them.[85] However, parties did not regain their leading position in transmitting political ideas to voters. The party's voice was one among many that simplified and clarified issues for the public—or, in opponents' views, distorted them.

Making Government Responsive to Public Opinion

The framers of the Constitution did not want the federal government to be too responsive to public opinion. Their ideal was government by wise, worthy, disinterested men elected by virtuous voters who then deferred to their judgment. The rise of parties and professional politicians dashed these hopes. Like most people, professional politicians hold some principles so dear that they will not violate them, but their first job is to get elected. To do that they must win votes, and they soon found that the best way to do it was by adhering to popular political ideologies and supporting popular programs that could best be articulated and advanced by organized parties. In fact, that was the best way to defeat elite, often better-known competitors, highly respected for their character.

The patronage system gave ordinary Americans a degree of power over the administration of government. Appointing and replacing government employees because of their political affiliations meant that the parties were responsible for how well employees did their jobs. The correspondence of congressmen and senators was filled with complaints from party activists when an appointee alienated locals by failing to fulfill his or her responsibilities. Such failures cost the party votes, they warned. Party leaders in

Washington carefully monitored such reports, as did leaders in state capitals with regard to state employees.[86]

Americans have always had ambivalent feelings about their reliance on professional politicians. They have always thought them short on expertise, principle, and integrity. Reformers pressed successfully to end the patronage system from the 1870s to the 1910s, hoping that the change would replace party hacks with professional civil servants.[87] It may have done so. But in the process ordinary Americans lost their ability to hold parties directly accountable for the quality of the government services they received. Reformers wanted to weaken party "machines" that relied on activists for manpower and funds, so that they would have to nominate men of character and ability (not yet women) in order to win elections. Instead, parties turned more and more to wealthy individuals and powerful interest groups for financial and political support, giving them more political influence than they had ever wielded before, and ordinary voters less.

V. THE INFLUENCE OF THE CONSTITUTION ON POLITICAL PARTIES

While parties would play a large role in developing the constitutional system, the system has also influenced the structure and behavior of political parties over time.

The Impact of the Federal System on Political Parties

The Constitution preserved a federal system in which most day-to-day government takes place at the state and local levels. It imposed no rules for the selection of state government officials other than requiring that states maintain republican forms of government. With few exceptions, Americans elected their aldermen and city councils, their mayors, state legislatures, other state officers, and even state and local judges. The candidates soon came to cooperate with candidates for other offices who shared the same political and constitutional principles. The consequence was that, unlike in most countries, in the United States successful political parties were organized from the bottom up. For much of American history, parties would remain decentralized, with weak national institutions and direction. Local partisans have regarded national parties as tools to help them win local elections as much as or more than representatives of national interests and ideologies. As a leading political scientist has observed, "The federal arrangement of the American system has produced a fragmented party system. Each of the fifty states has a separate party system, and underlying that system is a pattern of local interests, issues, and voting patterns. At the national level, the American party system is an amalgam of overlapping state, local, and regional interests."[88]

The framers of the Constitution expected that congressional delegations would represent state interests. Representation was apportioned by state. Senators were elected by state legislatures and later by the people of each state directly. The creation of national parties led to cross-state alliances based on economic interests and political and constitutional ideology. But local parties, responding to local interests, often resist the national party's legislative programs. Beholden to local interests and relying upon local voters, representatives and senators support national party programs that are unpopular with their constituents at their peril. Nonetheless, other factors, such as the desire to control the patronage and the fact that national electoral tides affect local elections, motivated state party leaders to work diligently for their national parties' electoral success in the nineteenth century. Local party conventions selected delegates to state conventions, which in turn selected delegates to national conventions. Because people tended to vote for the party rather than the candidate, local and state politicians had an interest in tailoring national candidates and platforms to help secure state and local victories. Every state had a representative on the platform committee, determined to secure a national platform that would rouse enthusiasm in his state. State conventions also named the state's representative to the party's national committee. State party platforms would stress those parts of the national party program that were most popular with state voters and downplay or ignore those that weren't.[89]

In the last decades of the nineteenth century, parties strengthened their national institutions, making their national committees more independent of state committees, although they were still made up of state-selected members. They raised and spent money independently of state organizations, sent out national campaign literature, and focused more on presidential than congressional campaigns. In the twentieth century, control of patronage waned as a motivation for state leaders to support their parties' national aspirations, and national political currents affected congressional and state elections less than they had earlier. But these motivations were replaced by equally compelling considerations. As the authority of the federal government grew in the twentieth century, its policies came to affect state interests profoundly. The federal government provided ever more financial resources to states and localities. State and local leaders continued to want the advantages that accrued when their political allies were in control of Washington. And they wanted officials who shared their economic philosophies and interests in charge of making and executing federal policy.

Local and state conventions continued to play an important role in party governance in the twentieth century, but under detailed rules states began to impose in its early decades. The laws of many states provided for conventions at several levels, with the most local selecting delegates to the next higher convention, and so on. This bottom-up structure assured that parties continued to press local interests on the center, rather than serving to impose the will of the center upon the locality.[90] In presidential primaries voters cast their ballots for national-convention delegates pledged to the candidate of their choice. Because delegates continued to be chosen state by state, presidential candidates continued to attend to every state's special interests and political profile.[91]

Equally important, the Constitution assigns the job of drawing congressional districts to the states. It is routine for dominant state parties to adjust the boundaries of congressional districts to maximize the number of people they can elect to the House of Representatives. Thus the balance of political forces in a state has always affected the partisan distribution of power in Washington. The state role in apportionment also adds to House members' reluctance to support national party policies that alienate voters back home. If the opposition gains control of the state, the representative might be redistricted out of his or her seat.

The Presidential Appointing Power and Political Parties

The Constitution gives the president the authority to nominate the officials who execute federal laws. In the nineteenth century, this ranged down to the level of local postmasters. President Andrew Jackson named local party activists to these offices, establishing the so-called patronage or "spoils" system. This helped tie the state and national levels of the political parties together. Controlling the presidency meant that state party activists would have access to federal appointments.[92] The constitutional custom of naming local residents to these offices made local opinion a strong constraint on the enforcement of federal laws, while the desire to obtain an office encouraged support of presidential policies. Cabinet members were chosen from important state leaders to represent their parties as much as to administer their departments. For a time, party appointments to government office were formalized to run through congressional representatives in some instances and through a state's U.S. senators in others. While the patronage system was slowly eliminated between the 1880s and the early twentieth century, presidents still depended on political allies to suggest appointees to the local political offices that remained at their disposal. His party's senators political allies in the U.S. Senate also continued to play a substantial role in the appointment of federal judges whose jurisdictions included their states, again bringing state interests to bear on an important area of public policy.[93]

The Electoral College and the Two-Party System

The Constitution provides that congressional and presidential elections be run state by state. Therefore presidential candidates and their parties have always tailored their campaigns to the interests and attitudes of state voters. This is especially true because presidents are not elected directly by the American people but through the Electoral College. To maximize its influence, nearly every state has provided that the electors pledged to the candidate who wins the most votes in the state will cast all the state's ballots in the Electoral College. As a consequence, presidential candidates and parties have skewed their nominations and platforms toward the most competitive states with the largest number of electoral votes. But it also has meant that parties and candidates have had to appeal to a broad range of states to win. Piling up huge margins in a few states would not secure victory in the Electoral College, even if it secured the majority of the popular vote.

The Electoral College has also contributed to establishing a two-party system rather than the multiparty system that characterizes many other nations. The constitutional custom of giving the winning candidate all the state's electoral votes created a strong incentive for smaller political organizations to combine in an effort to overtake the largest. Left free by the Constitution to devise their own election systems, nearly all states have established a process in which candidates for Congress and state offices could be elected by mere pluralities, paralleling the rules for selecting presidential electors. Most analysts believe that this "first past the post" constitutional custom is the most important factor in entrenching the two-party system.[94]

Regulation of Parties, and Its Constitutional Limits

The Constitution gives Congress the power to alter state regulations of "the times, places and manner for holding elections for Senators and Representatives" (U.S. Constitution, Art. I, sec. 4). The Supreme Court has interpreted that power broadly, holding that the federal government has the inherent power to protect the integrity of federal elections. It has also implied that the federal government has the power to regulate parties under the Fourteenth and Fifteenth Amendments, which guarantee civil and political rights. In 1944 it held that rules limiting participation in party primary elections to whites were unconstitutional.[95] Since both amendments authorize congressional enforcement of their provisions, the Court's ruling implied that the federal government had the power to assure that party rules afford due process and equal protection to all. But despite this broad authority, Congress has been slow to regulate political parties directly. It did not do so until 1972.

Parties were instead subject to intensive state regulation.[96] The process began in the late nineteenth century. The first state regulations, passed in the 1870s, governed the size, shape, and color of the tickets that parties distributed to voters to be placed in ballot boxes. The idea was to stop party activists from confirming that bribed voters actually deposited brightly colored, easily observed ballots in the ballot box. In the 1880s states began to mandate the use of standard, state-printed ballots, to be cast secretly instead of openly. Then important legislation went to the heart of party operations: states required parties to select candidates through direct primary elections rather than party conventions and caucuses. Beginning in the South in the 1880s and 1890s as a way to marginalize black voters, the system spread North in the 1900s. From these initial interventions in party processes, the states would develop a complex body of regulations governing nearly all aspects of party organization, so fundamental that they have become part of the customary constitution. The regulations were designed to democratize the parties—to reduce the influence of party leaders and increase the influence of ordinary voters. It was, in the words of one scholar, "the revival of the Constitution-against-Parties."[97]

National and state party leaders cooperated in these reforms. Government had become too complex to be staffed by people chosen primarily for their political services and subject to politically motivated removal regardless of their expertise. Determining whom to appoint had become an intolerable burden on the senators who had benefited from the system for so long. Caucuses and conventions had become too difficult to manage, providing power bases for recalcitrant local politicians. Party leaders' interests and those of reformers coincided to inaugurate changes that over time would seriously weaken political parties in the United States.

The constitutionality of these new regulations was tested in state courts. Because the rule at the time was that the Bill of Rights restricted only federal action, challengers argued that the regulations violated state constitutional guarantees of freedom of association. But state courts upheld nearly all the laws. Parties had become so central to constitutional democracy that they were recast, in the words of an analyst, "from private voluntary associations controlling their own internal procedures to quasi-state agencies regulated to serve public political interests." Judges proved to be "enthusiastic partners" of legislatures "in the transformation of political parties."[98]

Congress limited itself to regulating campaign finances—barring corporations and unions from contributing money to campaigns, and limiting campaign spending, requiring disclosure of contributions. The Supreme Court upheld these laws against various challenges.[99] Congress did not directly regulate political parties until it passed the Federal Election Campaign Act of 1972,[100] which regulated campaign spending and created a Federal Elections Commission (FEC) to issue further guidelines. The law reflected radical changes in the role parties played in the political system by the mid-twentieth century. By then, parties no longer monopolized campaigns, having been augmented and even replaced by the independent media, political action committees (PACs) established by all sorts of special interests, and the institutions candidates developed to finance and run their campaigns independently of their parties. Analysts referred to a "transformation in American politics" and wondered whether parties were in terminal decline.[101]

The 1972 law mandated contribution limits on political donations to the national party committees, individual candidates, and PACs for use in federal elections. It limited how much candidates, PACs, and the parties' national committees could spend on candidates' campaigns for federal office. The law also enabled presidential candidates to secure public financing for their primary and general election campaigns, in return for accepting limits on expenditures. While structured to limit the benefits to the candidates of the two major parties, the money went to the candidates' treasuries rather than the parties', exacerbating the shift from party to candidate in the political process.

In 1976 the Supreme Court ruled that the law's limits on spending by PACs and individuals unconstitutionally limited their freedom of speech. But the justices at first left in place the law's limits on party expenditures, potentially further eroding the parties' role in the political process.[102] The FEC responded by taking steps to loosen the restrictions. It interpreted the law in a way that freed "soft money" to be spent on things other than candidates' campaigns. In 1996 the Supreme Court reinforced the trend by ruling that spending limits on party activities unconnected to specific candidates were unconstitutional infringements of freedom of speech.[103] Although the Supreme Court upheld limits on party spending that was coordinated with candidates,[104] for all practical purposes the parties and interest groups had gotten around the law.

Most of the party activities supported by "soft money"—money not directly spent on candidates' campaigns—were undertaken by the party national committees, because provisions of the law hampered state and local party committees from doing the same things. This strengthened the national party committees relative to those of the states. By the 1980s an analyst referred to national party organizations as "The New Giants."[105] As parties became ideologically coherent in the 1990s, they became more attractive conduits for exercising influence on public opinion and public policy. The exemption of so many party activities from spending limits encouraged an outpouring of money, which parties indirectly used to help candidates wage their campaigns within the loose confines of the law. The combination of ideological consistency and money tied candidates more closely to their parties than they had been in decades.[106]

In 2002 Congress tried to close the loopholes with the McCain-Feingold Act, which tried to staunch the flow of interest-group money into party coffers, restricted how parties could spend "soft money," and barred corporations, union, and independent PACS from making any kind of "electioneering statement" that supported or opposed candidates for federal office by name during the election season.[107] At first the Supreme Court upheld the law, but in 2010 it ruled in *Citizens United v. FEC* that Congress could not constitutionally prevent corporations, unions, and nonprofit organizations from paying for independent electioneering statements.[108] More significantly, it severely narrowed the basis for any restrictions on political contributions. Soon thereafter the lower federal courts relied on *Citizens United* to rule that Congress could not limit contributions to PACs that were independent of parties and candidates.[109] The Court soon found state laws regulating campaign finances unconstitutional as well.[110] While corporations have been slow to take advantage, the controversial decisions opened elections to a torrent of unregulated money that had to be raised and spent outside party structures and control, apparently once again privileging nonparty political activity over party activities. By 2011 supporters of particular candidates were establishing "Super PACs" that could collect and spend unlimited amounts of money to back their favorites and attack their opponents, as long as they did not explicitly coordinate their activities directly with the candidates or the parties.[111] In 2015 they were collecting tens of millions to spend on behalf of candidates for the Republican and Democratic presidential nominations. Ideologically oriented PACs joined the fray. In the elections of 2012 and 2014 unprecedented floods of unregulated money cascaded into states with closely contested races.[112]

The effect on parties remains uncertain. Some analysts say they are stronger than ever.[113] Others suggest that Super PACs may develop into strongly ideological entities working outside and at odds with out-financed political parties.[114] In *McCutcheon v. FEC* (2014), however, the Supreme Court overturned the aggregate limits statutes imposed on contributions to candidates and the national parties, putting them on a more even footing with PACs in seeking contributions. Then Congress strengthened party fundraising further, raising the limit that individuals could contribute to national party committees from $32,400 to $324,000 per year.

PACs and parties are not necessarily competitors. In the general elections of 2012 and 2014, the supposedly independent activities of PACs and parties in fact seemed to be rather well coordinated in terms of themes and locations of expenditures. Rarely did parties and PACs appear to be in competition.[115] But PACs have helped conservative candidates challenge less extreme Republicans in that party's primaries. Successful insurgents have proved more difficult to unite behind party positions in legislatures. Ideologically driven PACs have combined with conservative Tea Party activists to drive the Republican Party farther to the right than the electorate. These factors have created tensions between far-right activists and mainstream Republicans.[116]

The Supreme Court and Political Parties

For most of American history, the Supreme Court avoided considering the place of political parties in the constitutional system. The exception arose when the Court overturned state laws and party rules that allowed only whites to vote in Democratic Party primaries. In those cases, the justices stressed the circumstances in which political parties fulfilled essentially state functions.[117] The decisions reinforced the tendency of state courts to treat parties as public utilities subject to wide-ranging state regulation.

The Supreme Court became more willing to evaluate the constitutionality of regulations affecting parties in the mid-twentieth century, as Americans looked more and more to courts for the resolution of constitutional issues. Political parties are connected to a number of rights guaranteed in the Constitution. The First Amendment protects freedom of association, especially for political purposes, but it also protects freedom of speech, and the Fourteenth Amendment guarantees equal protection of the laws. Issues involving these rights were raised both by government regulation of parties and the rules that parties themselves established, sometimes bringing different rights into conflict. The justices considered whether states could impose rules for selecting delegates to national party conventions that were inconsistent with the rules set by the national parties themselves. They pondered how far states could go in imposing rules on party primaries. When state legislatures made it difficult for minor parties to get on the ballot, the justices struggled to decide how high they could constitutionally raise the bar. When party rules seemed to infringe on individual rights or the equal rights of minority groups, the justices labored to balance such traditional concerns with the right of political associations to order their affairs free of government interference.[118]

In contrast to state decisions that continued to find a wide scope for state regulations, the justices perceived such regulations as infringing the right to associate freely for political purposes. Such infringements could be justified only to serve compelling state interests. Applying that rule, the justices held that national party rules governing who could be seated at national conventions superseded inconsistent state laws.[119] They ruled that states could not mandate that voting in primaries be limited to party members if the parties wanted them open to all. Nor could states force primaries to be open if the parties wanted them closed. The Court overturned laws forbidding state parties from endorsing candidates in primary elections.[120] While it ruled that there were limits to how far states could go to discourage minor parties' access to the ballot, it more often held that the states' interest in orderly elections trumped the right of small parties to such access.[121] By the 1990s legal analysts discerned a pattern: the justices seemed to be reinforcing the two-party system, in effect recognizing the central role the two parties played in the American constitutional system.

Still, there were signs of ambivalence. The Court upheld a number of regulations of parties that were designed to prevent corruption, or even the appearance of corruption, in the political process. When it initially upheld the McCain-Feingold Act in 2003, the narrow (5-4) majority echoed the traditional suspicion that political parties corrupt politics. "The idea that large contributions to a national party can corrupt or, at the very least, create the appearance of corruption of federal candidates and officeholders is neither novel nor implausible," they observed. National parties were "in a unique position . . . to serve as 'agents for spending on behalf of those who seek to produce obligated officeholders.' . . . [R]ather than resist that role, the national parties have actively embraced it."[122]

Chief Justice William H. Rehnquist's dissent expressed a different view. Parties were more than political machines serving ambitious politicians, he wrote. They "are exemplars of political speech at all levels of government." They "promote coordinated political messages and participate in public policy debates . . . . [P]olitical parties often foster speech crucial to a healthy democracy and fulfill the need for like-minded individuals to band together and promote a political philosophy."[123] For Rehnquist, political parties were part of an amorphous process in which public opinion is translated into public policy—what legal scholar Robert Post calls "discursive democracy."[124] The Court's decisions in the *Citizens United* and *McCutcheon* cases seemed to reflect Rehnquist's exaltation of political parties as a medium for the dissemination of ideas rather than an instrument of government. As another analyst has put it, when it comes to regulating political campaigns, the Court posits "A Free Speech (Only) Constitution."[125] If so, the Supreme Court will view state and federal regulations of political parties as limitations of free speech, requiring stricter judicial scrutiny than they have faced in the past.

EPILOGUE: POLITICAL PARTIES AND THE CONSTITUTION

Political parties have played a central role in raising and deciding constitutional issues in American history. Although the courts, especially the United States Supreme Court, have been the primary forum for establishing constitutional law, that law reflects the decisions American voters have made about constitutional policy. For most of our history that has been the main way in which constitutional policy has been established. Only since the mid-twentieth century have the Supreme Court's determinations of constitutional law seemed to displace that popular authority. This process is neither complete nor irreversible. If there is a revival of popular constitutionalism, political parties are sure once again to play a key role in articulating constitutional issues and providing a way for the American people to decide them.

FURTHER READING

Although constitutional historians once took a broad view of the Constitution, during the second half of the twentieth century they, like political scientists and legal academics, tended to focus their attention on the history of constitutional law as exposited by the Supreme Court. This began to change in the 1990s as legal scholars in many fields began to explore how court doctrines were affected by political, social, and intellectual forces outside their chambers, and how non-judicial actors determined the contours of the constitutional system.

Mark Tushnet discusses the "Constitution Outside the Constitution" in *Why the Constitution Matters* (New Haven, Conn.: Yale University Press, 2010). In a series of essays, Keith E. Whittington describes what he calls "the political constitution" in *Constitutional Construction: Divided Powers and Constitutional Meaning* (Cambridge, Mass.: Harvard University Press, 1999). H. Jefferson Powell has done something similar in *A Community Built on Words: The Constitution in History and Politics* (Chicago: University of Chicago Press, 2002). The essays in *Constitutional Politics: Essays on Constitution Making, Maintenance, and Change*, ed. Sotirios A. Barber and Robert P. George (Princeton, N.J.: Princeton University Press, 2001), likewise conceive of the Constitution as more than mere constitutional law. Perhaps the most ambitious effort to distinguish between what he calls the "Civic Constitution" and the "Juridic Constitution" is John E. Finn's *Peopling the Constitution* (Lawrence: University Press of Kansas, 2014). However, Finn does not formally explicate the role of political parties in maintaining the Civic Constitution.

Although there has been relatively little attention paid to the role the parties themselves have played in American constitutional development, there has been a good deal of study devoted to the relationship between constitutional law and politics in general, especially to the role courts play in different political/constitutional "regimes." Michael McCann puts the Supreme Court's decisions in the context of a larger constitutional politics in "How the Supreme Court Matters in American Politics: New Institutionalist Perspectives," in *The Supreme Court in American Politics: New Institutionalist Interpretations*, ed. Howard Gillman and Cornell Clayton (Lawrence: University Press of Kansas, 1999), 63–97. Stephen

Griffin takes a theoretical approach in *American Constitutionalism: From Theory to Politics* (Princeton, N.J.: Princeton University Press, 1996).

But legal analysts have paid scant attention to incorporating parties themselves into constitutional theory. Michael A. Fitts tries to explain why in "Back to the Future: The Enduring Dilemmas Revealed in the Supreme Court's Treatment of Political Parties," in *The U.S. Supreme Court and the Electoral Process*, 2nd ed., ed. David K. Ryden (Washington, D.C.: Georgetown University Press, 2002). John Epperson discusses the radical expansion of state regulation of parties in the late nineteenth and twentieth centuries, as well the judicial reaction in *The Changing Legal Status of Political Parties in the United States* (New York: Garland, Publishing, 1986). Three essays, making up Section Two of *The U.S. Supreme Court and the Electoral Process*, address the Supreme Court's struggle to define the place of political parties in the constitutional system.

Rather than developing a theoretical understanding of the role of parties in the constitutional system, legal scholars have concentrated on relating developments in constitutional law to changes in political/constitutional "regimes." See, for examples, Howard Gillman, "Courts and the Politics of Partisan Coalitions," in *The Oxford Handbook of Law and Politics*, ed. Keith E. Whittington et al. (New York: Oxford University Press, 2008); John J. Janssen, *Constitutional Equilibria: The Partisan Contingency of American Constitutional Law from the Jeffersonian "Revolution" to the Impeachment of Bill Clinton* (Lanham, Md.: University Press of America, 2000); Gerard N. Magliocca, *Andrew Jackson and the Constitution: The Rise and Fall of Generational Regimes* (Lawrence: University Press of Kansas, 2007); and Keith E. Whittington, *Political Foundations of Judicial Supremacy: The Presidency, the Supreme Court, and Constitutional Leadership in U.S. History* (Princeton, N.J.: Princeton University Press, 2007). This idea is related to the concept of "partisan realignment" that political scientists developed in the mid-twentieth century to explain major political changes in American history. For overviews, read Jerome M. Clubb et al., *Partisan Realignment: Voters, Parties, and Government in American History* (Boulder, Colo.: Westview Press, 1990); Joel H. Silbey, "The Rise and Fall of American Political Parties, 1790–1993," in *The Parties Respond: Changes in American Parties and Campaigns*, ed. L. Sandy Maisel, 2nd ed. (Boulder, Colo.: Westview, 1994), 3–20; James L. Sundquist, *Dynamics of the Party System; Alignment and Realignment of Political Parties in the United States* (Washington, D.C.: Brookings Institution, 1973); and Richard M. Yon, "Critical Realignment Theory," in *The Encyclopedia of Political Science*, ed. George Thomas Kurian (Washington, D.C: CQ Press, 2011).

The notions of "regime change" and "partisan realignment" inherently implicate political parties. Every study of constitutional regime change does mention the political parties involved, and Tushnet acknowledges the centrality of political parties to the Constitution in *Why the Constitution Matters*. Yet not much scholarly work has explored the constitutional aspect of party ideologies. John Gerring, *Party Ideologies in America, 1828–1996* (New York: Cambridge University Press, 1998) subsumes constitutional ideologies under "statism" in the case of Republicans and under numerous headings, such as limited government, preserving liberty, and majority rule and minority rights, in the case of the Democrats. In *Federalism and the Making of America* (New York: Routledge, 2012), David Brian Robertson discusses the effect of federalism issues on party formation and organization. Elvin T. Lim sees the two major parties as representing two competing visions of federalism that have characterized American history. See Lim, *The Lovers' Quarrel: The Two Foundings and American Political Development* (New York: Oxford University Press, 2014). General histories of the political parties often mention constitutional issues, but none makes them central to their story. See, for example, A. James Reichley, *The Life of the Parties: A History of American Political Parties* (New York: The Free Press, 1992). Esposito comes closest in *Pragmatism, Politics, and Perversity: Democracy and the American Party Battle* (Lanham, Md.: Lexington Books, 2012), a neo-Beardian interpretation of political history, but he rarely cites conservative parties' constitutional arguments among the many hypocrisies he attributes to them.

In fact, the influential political scientist Theodore J. Lowi discounts the influence of parties on the substance of American constitutional policy, arguing that their constitutional role has consisted primarily in legitimizing political decisions. See Lowi, "Party, Policy, and Constitution in America," in *The American Party System: Stages of Development* (New York: Oxford University Press, 1975). John Zvesper argues that there is actually a tension between political parties and constitutional government, in that parties provide a vehicle through which the people override the constraints that the Constitution was intended to impose on their power. See John Zvesper, "American Political Parties and Constitutional Government," in *Reflections on the Constitution: The American Constitution after Two Hundred Years*, ed. Richard Maidment and John Zvesper (Manchester, U.K..: Manchester University Press, 1989).

In preparing this essay, I have gleaned information from a wide variety of sources that discuss aspects of political party history, organization, practices, and customs. The standard academic survey of political parties is Paul Allen

Beck and Marjorie Randon Hershey, *Party Politics in America*, now in its
14th edition (New York: Longman, 2011). It does not directly address the
relationship between the Constitution and parties, but provides a wealth
of information related to changes over time in the structure and operation
of parties, their role in politics and policy making, and their regulation.
See also Leon D. Epstein, *Political Parties in the American Mold* (Madison:
University of Wisconsin Press, 1986), which has a much more substantial
but now somewhat dated discussion of the legal status of parties. One
can learn about parties and political practices over time from such works
as Glenn C. Altschuler and Stuart M. Blumin, *Rude Republic: Americans
and Their Politics in the Nineteenth Century* (Princeton, N.J.: Princeton
University Press, 2000); Richard F. Bensel, *The American Ballot Box in the
Mid-Nineteenth Century* (New York: Cambridge University Press, 2004);
and Robert J. Dinkin, *Campaigning in America: A History of Election
Practices* (New York: Greenwood, 1989), 11–30. Stephen Skowronek,
*Building a New American State: The Expansion of National Administrative
Capacities, 1877–1920* (New York: Cambridge University Press, 1982), and
Richard F. Bensel, *Yankee Leviathan: The Origins of Central State Authority
in America, 1859–1877* (New York: Cambridge University Press, 1990)
are crucial to understanding the general role of parties in the nineteenth-
century American state and how that role changed in the transition to
the modern, administrative state. For the impact of federalism on party
structure and activities, see David Brian Robertson, "Federalism, Political
Parties, and Interests," in his *Federalism and the Making of America* (New
York: Routledge, 2012). For party organization, structure, and the role of
patronage, one can consult James S. Chase, *Emergence of the Presidential
Nominating Convention 1789–1832* (Urbana: University of Illinois Press,
1973); Daniel Klinghard, *The Nationalization of American Political Parties,
1880–1896* (New York: Cambridge University Press, 2010); John F.
Reynolds, *The Demise of the American Convention System, 1880–1911* (New
York: Cambridge University Press, 2006); Ari Hoogenboom, *Outlawing the
Spoils: A History of the Civil Service Reform Movement, 1865–1883* (Urbana:
University of Illinois Press, 1961); Anne Freeman, *Patronage: An American
Tradition* (Chicago: Nelson-Hall, 1994); C. K. Yearley, *The Money
Machines: The Breakdown and Reform of Governmental and Party Finance in
the North, 1860–1920* (Albany: State University of New York Press, 1970).

Changes in the era of the Internet are coming so quickly that scholarly
studies of parties cannot keep up with them. John C. Green and Daniel
J. Coffey (eds.), *The State of the Parties: People, Passions, and Power*, 6th
ed. (Lanham, Md.: Rowman and Littlefield, 2011); James A. Thurber
and Candice J. Nelson (eds.), *Campaigns and Elections American Style:*

Transforming American Politics, 4th ed. (Boulder, Colo.: Westview Press, 2014); and the 14th edition of Beck and Hershey, *Politics in America*, mentioned above, will all need quick and constant updates. The Supreme Court's dismantling of the regulations governing campaign finance has created a large legal and political science literature. Among the most insightful are Robert C. Post's *Citizens Divided: Campaign Finance Reform and the Constitution* (Cambridge, Mass.: Harvard University Press, 2014) and Zephyr Teachout, *Corruption in America: From Benjamin Franklin's Snuff Box to Citizens United* (Cambridge, Mass.: Harvard University Press, 2014).

The classic exposition of the Founders' attitude toward faction and parties is Gordon Wood, *The Creation of the American Republic, 1776–1787* (Chapel Hill: University of North Carolina Press, 1969). Richard Hofstadter's equally seminal *The Idea of a Party System: The Rise of Legitimate Opposition in the United States, 1780–1840* (Berkeley: University of California Press, 1969) is the standard account of how parties came to be seen as legitimate elements of the constitutional system. John H. Aldrich presents an elegant explanation of the factors that would lead politicians to establish political parties in any republican system of government in *Why Parties? The Origin and Transformation of Political Parties in America* (Chicago: University of Chicago Press, 1995). Wood's *Empire of Liberty: A History of the Early Republic, 1789–1815* (New York: Oxford University Press, 2009) describes the organization of the Federalist and Republican Parties and the centrality of constitutional issues to their development. Gerald Leonard demonstrates how central constitutional commitments were to the legitimization of political parties in *The Invention of Party Politics: Federalism, Popular Sovereignty, and Constitutional Development in Jacksonian Illinois* (Chapel Hill: University of North Carolina Press, 2002). Even more to the point is his essay "Party as a 'Political Safeguard of Federalism': Martin Van Buren and the Constitutional Theory of Party Politics," *Rutgers Law Review* 54 (Fall 2001): 221–81.

A number of constitutional historians, political scientists, and legal academics have looked at constitutional issues in specific partisan eras. However, in some cases one still must glean those issues from more general accounts. For constitutional issues in the first party era, see Bruce Ackerman, *The Failure of the Founding Fathers: Jefferson, Marshall, and the Rise of Presidential Democracy* (Cambridge, Mass.: Harvard University Press, 2005); Michael Les Benedict, "The Jeffersonian Republicans and American Liberty," in *Essays on the History of Liberty: Seaver Institute Lectures at the Huntington Library* (San Marino, Calif.: Huntington Library, 1989), 23–41; and Gordon Wood, *Empire of Liberty*. For the constitutional issues of the Jacksonian era, read Gerard N. Magliocca, *Andrew Jackson and the Constitution*; Robert Remini, *Andrew Jackson and the Bank War: A Study in the Growth of Presidential Power* (New York: W. W. Norton, 1967); Robert Remini, "The Constitution and the Presidencies: The Jackson Era," in *The Constitution and the American Presidency*, ed. Martin Fausold and Alan Shank (Albany: State University of New York Press, 1991), 29–44; Richard E. Ellis, *The Union at Risk: Jacksonian Democracy, States' Rights, and the Nullification Crisis* (New York: Oxford University Press, 1987). In his majestic *What Hath God Wrought: The Transformation of America, 1815–1848* (New York: Oxford University Press, 2007), Daniel Walker Howe contrasts Whig modernizers and Jacksonian traditionalists. Although he relates this disagreement to different interpretations of the Constitution, he does not stress the constitutional aspects of his panorama. But the way these rival constellations of ideas related to constitutional disputes is clear.

For the constitutional politics of the third (Civil War/Reconstruction/ Industrialization) party period, see Michael Les Benedict, *Preserving the Constitution: Essays on Politics and the Constitution in the Reconstruction Era* (New York: Fordham University Press, 2006); Michael Les Benedict, "Law and the Constitution in the Gilded Age," in *The Gilded Age: Perspectives on the Origins of Modern America*, 2nd ed., ed. Charles W. Calhoun (Lanham, Md.: Rowman & Littlefield, 2006), 333–51; Arthur M. Bestor, "The American Civil War as a Constitutional Crisis," *American Historical Review* 69 (January 1964): 327–52; Williamjames Hoffer, *To Enlarge the Machinery of Government: Congressional Debates and the Growth of the American State, 1858–1891* (Baltimore, Md.: Johns Hopkins University Press, 2007); Harold M. Hyman and William M. Wiecek, *Equal Justice Under Law: Constitutional Development, 1835–1875* (New York: Harper & Row, 1982); Harold M. Hyman, *A More Perfect Union: The Impact of the Civil War and Reconstruction on the Constitution* (New York: Oxford University Press, 1973); Joel Silbey, *A Respectable Minority: The Democratic Party in the Civil War Era, 1860–1868* (New York: W. W. Norton, 1977). For the abortive Populist challenge to the declining regime, see Gerard N. Magliocca, *The Tragedy of William Jennings Bryan: Constitutional Law and the Politics of Backlash* (New Haven, Conn.: Yale University Press, 2011).

For the Progressive Era, see John A. Marini and Ken Masugi, eds., *The Progressive Revolution in Politics and Political Science: Transforming the American Regime* (Lanham, Md.: Rowman & Littlefield, 2005), which proceeds from a conservative normative position but describes the essence of Progressive constitutional ideas; William H. Harbaugh, "The Constitution of the Theodore Roosevelt Presidency and the Progressive Era," in *The Constitution and the American Presidency*, ed. Martin L. Fausold and Alan

Shank (Albany: State University of New York Press, 1991); John A. Rohr, *To Run a Constitution: The Legitimacy of the Administrative State* (Lawrence: University Press of Kansas, 1986). On the constitutional politics of the New Deal, consult Bruce Ackerman, "Modernity," in Ackerman, *We the People*, Vol. 2: *Transformations* (Cambridge, Mass.: Harvard University Press, 1998); Alan Brinkley, "The New Deal and the Idea of the State," in *The Rise and Fall of the New Deal Order*, ed. Steve Fraser and Gary Gerstle (Princeton, N.J.: Princeton University Press, 1989); Marian C. McKenna, *Franklin Roosevelt and the Great Constitutional War: The Court-Packing Crisis of 1937* (New York: Fordham University Press, 2002); Michael E. Parrish, "The Great Depression, the New Deal, and the American Legal Order," *Washington Law Review* 59 (October 1983): 723–50. On the constitutional issues of the Civil Rights regime, see Hugh Davis Graham, *The Civil Rights Era: Origins and Development of National Policy, 1960–1972* (New York: Oxford University Press, 1990); Harvard Sitkoff, *The Struggle for Black Equality, 1954–1980* (New York: Hill and Wang, 1981); Donald G. Nieman, "The Civil Rights Movement and American Law, 1950–1969," in *Promises to Keep: African-Americans and the Constitutional Order, 1776 to the Present* (New York: Oxford University Press, 1991), 147–88; Sandra F. VanBurkleo, "The Civil Rights Settlement," in *"Belonging to the World": Women's Rights and American Constitutional Culture* (New York: Oxford University Press, 2001). For the growing role of courts in determining constitutional policy in the Civil Rights partisan era, see Ran Hirschl, "The Judicialization of Politics," in *The Oxford Handbook of Law and Politics*, 119–41, and Lawrence Baum, "Supreme Court Activism and the Constitution," in *The Constitution and American Political Development*, ed. Peter F. Nardulli (Urbana: University of Illinois Press, 1992). Mark Tushnet places the Warren Court in the context of ascendant liberalism in "The Warren Court as History: An Interpretation," in *The Warren Court in Historical and Political Perspective*, ed. Mark Tushnet (Charlottesville: University Press of Virginia, 1993).

For the growing divergence in the constitutional philosophies of the Republican and Democratic Parties in the conservative partisan era, see Thomas Byrne Edsall and Mary D. Edsall, *Chain Reaction: The Impact of Race, Rights, and Taxes on American Politics* (New York: W. W. Norton, 1992); James Davison Hunter, *Culture Wars: The Struggle to Define America* (New York: Basic Books, 1991); Matthew Levendusky, *The Partisan Sort: How Liberals Became Democrats and Conservatives Became Republicans* (Chicago: University of Chicago Press, 2009); Bruce Nesmith, *The New Republican Coalition: The Reagan Campaigns and White Evangelicals* (New York: P. Lang, 1994).

ENDNOTES

1. For an accessible description of various aspects of the "constitution," see Mark Tushnet, *Why the Constitution Matters* (New Haven, Conn.: Yale University Press, 2010), 1–17.

2. Keith E. Whittington, *Constitutional Construction: Divided Powers and Constitutional Meaning* (Cambridge, Mass.: Harvard University Press, 1999), 1.

3. Constitutional scholars Robert Post and Reva B. Siegel call this power to influence courts "democratic constitutionalism." See Post and Siegel, "Democratic Constitutionalism," in *The Constitution in 2020*, ed. Jack M. Balkin and Reva B. Seigel (New York: Oxford University Press, 2009), 25-34.

4. Wayne Moore, *Constitutional Rights and Powers of the People* (Princeton, N.J.: Princeton University Press, 1996), 1.

5. John Adams, *The Papers of John Adams*, ed. Robert J. Taylor et al. (Cambridge, Mass.: Harvard University Press, 1977), 1: 77; George Washington, *The Writings of George Washington*, ed. John C. Fitzhugh (Washington, D.C.: Government Printing Office, 1931–1944), 35: 226. The classic discussions of the Founders' attitudes toward parties and factions are Gordon Wood, *The Creation of the American Republic, 1776–1789* (Chapel Hill: University of North Carolina Press, 1969), and Richard Hofstadter, *The Idea of a Party System: The Rise of Legitimate Opposition in the United States, 1780–1840* (Berkeley: University of California Press, 1969).

6. Washington, *Writings*, 35: 226; Washington to Henry Knox, December 26, 1786, ibid., 29: 122; James Madison, *Federalist No. 10*, in Alexander Hamilton, James Madison, and John Jay, *The Federalist Papers*, ed. Clinton Rossiter (New York: New American Library, 2003), 71. Charles Lee to Robert Morris, August 15, 1782, in "Lee Papers, 1782–1811," *Collections of the New York Historical Society* 4 (1874): 26–27 (spelling as in original).

7. Lee to Morris, August 15, 1782, in "Lee Papers," 27; George Washington to Henry Knox, December 26, 1786, in *Writings of Washington*, 29: 122.

8. *The Debates in the Several State Conventions on the Adoption of the Constitution*, ed. Jonathan Elliot (Philadelphia: Jonathan Elliott, 1836), 2: 320.

9. Madison, *Federalist No. 10*, in *The Federalist Papers*, 76, 71, 79, respectively.

10. The following discussion is based on classic accounts of the development of national political parties in the decade following the Constitution's ratification: Hofstadter, *The Idea of a Party System*; Bruce Ackerman, *The Failure of the Founding Fathers: Jefferson, Marshall, and the Rise of Presidential Democracy* (Cambridge, Mass.: Harvard University Press, 2005); Morton Borden, *Parties and Politics in the Early Republic, 1789–1815* (London: Routledge & K. Paul, 1968); Noble E. Cunningham, *The Jeffersonian Republicans: The Formation of Party Organization, 1789–1801* (Chapel Hill: University of North Carolina Press, 1957); Gordon Wood, *Empire of Liberty: A History of the Early Republic, 1789–1815* (New York: Oxford University Press, 2009); Eric L. McKitrick and Stanley M. Elkins, *The Age of Federalism: The Early American Republic, 1788-1800* (New York: Oxford University Press, 1993).

11. Thomas Jefferson, *Opinion on the Constitutionality of a National Bank*, in *The Writings of Thomas Jefferson*, ed. Paul Leicester Ford (New York: G. P. Putnam's Sons, 1892-1899), 5: 284-89.

12. Alexander Hamilton, *Opinion as to the Constitutionality of the Bank of the United States*, in *The Works of Alexander Hamilton*, ed. Henry Cabot Lodge (New York: G. P. Putnam's Sons, 1904), 3: 445–94.

13. Quoted in Hofstadter, *The Idea of a Party System*, 95.

14. Robert J. Dinkin, *Campaigning in America: A History of Election Practices* (New York: Greenwood, 1989), 11–30; Jeffrey L. Pasley, "The Cheese and the Words: Popular Political Culture and Participatory Democracy in the Early American Republic," in *Beyond the Founders: New Approaches to the Political History of the Early American Republic*, ed. Jeffrey L. Pasley et al. (Chapel Hill: University of North Carolina Press, 2004), 31–56.

15. See Michael Les Benedict, "The Jeffersonian Republicans and American Liberty," in *Essays on the History of Liberty: Seaver Institute Lectures at the Huntington Library* (San Marino, Calif.: Huntington Library, 1989), 23–41.

16. *U.S. Statutes at Large*, 1: 596 (July 14, 1798). For the constitutional controversy surrounding the Alien and Sedition Acts, see James M. Smith, *Freedom's Fetters: The Alien and Sedition Laws and American Civil Liberties* (Ithaca, N.Y.: Cornell University Press, 1956) and Charles Slack, *Liberty's First Crisis: Adams, Jefferson, and the Misfits Who Saved Free Speech* (New York: Atlantic Monthly Press, 2015).

17. James Madison, "A Candid State of Parties," in *The Writings of James Madison . . .* , ed. Gaillard Hunt (New York: G. P. Putnam's Sons, 1900),

6:106–19, quoted at 114; Jefferson to John Taylor, June 1, 1798, in *Works of Thomas Jefferson*, 8: 431.

18. Bruce Ackerman makes this point especially well in his *Failure of the Founding Fathers*, 80–92.

19. Thomas Jefferson, *First Inaugural Address*, in *A Compilation of the Messages and Papers of the Presidents, 1789–1897*, ed. James D. Richardson (Washington, D.C.: Government Printing Office, 1896–1897), 1: 321–24.

20. Andrew E. Busch, *The Constitution on the Campaign Trail: The Surprising Career of America's Founding Document* (Lanham, Md.: Rowman & Littlefield, 2007).

21. In the late 1980s, 60 percent of respondents said the Supreme Court was "the final authority on the interpretation of the Constitution." Busch, *Constitution on the Campaign Trail*, 211.

22. Cooper v. Aaron, 358 U.S. 1 (1958); City of Boerne v. Flores, 521 U.S. 507 (1997). See Larry D. Kramer, "Foreword: We the Court," *Harvard Law Review* 115 (November 2001): 4–169, at 128–60. Of course, the Court's decisions must command popular respect. But that respect results in "the people's acceptance of the Judiciary as fit to determine what the National law means, and to declare what it demands." Planned Parenthood v. Casey, 505 U.S. 833, at 865.

23. See, for example, the discussion of these problems in the context of the right of a woman to choose to have an abortion in *Planned Parenthood v. Casey*, at 854–69.

24. Political scientists do not agree about the appropriate term to describe eras of U.S. history characterized by different party structures, voting behavior, issues, and policy outcomes. The term "party system" is associated with the idea that new eras have been introduced by critical elections, in which new voting patterns emerged. Over time, the nature of the eras that followed such elections came to be seen as more important than the elections themselves. The last critical election occurred in 1932, however. Since it is clear that there have been major changes in all the other indices of party eras since that time, some political scientists and legal scholars speak of partisan or political "regimes"—a broader notion than a party system or party era. See Scott Barclay and Susan S. Silbey, "Understanding Regime Change: Public Opinion, Legitimacy, and Legal Consciousness," in *The Oxford Handbook of Law and Politics*, ed. Keith E. Whittington et al. (New York: Oxford University Press, 2008), 663–78; Howard Gillman, "Courts and the Politics of Partisan Coalitions," ibid., 644–62. I will use the terms more or less interchangeably. For a discussion of how the terms developed,

see A. J. Polsky, "The Political Economy of Partisan Regimes: Lessons from Two Republican Eras," *Polity* 25 (July 2003): 595–612.

25. Walter Dean Burnham, *Critical Elections and the Mainsprings of American Politics* (New York: W. W. Norton, 1970); Jerome M. Clubb et al., *Partisan Realignment: Voters, Parties, and Government in American History* (Boulder, Colo.: Westview Press, 1990); Dean McSweeney and John Zvesper, *American Political Parties: The Formation, Decline and Reform of the American Party System* (London & New York: Routledge, 1991); James L. Sundquist, *Dynamics of the Party System: Alignment and Realignment of Political Parties in the United States* (Washington, D.C.: Brookings Institution, 1984).

26. Gerald Leonard, "Party as a 'Political Safeguard of Federalism': Martin Van Buren and the Constitutional Theory of Party Politics," *Rutgers Law Review* 54 (Fall 2001): 221–81; Lynn Hudson Parsons, *The Birth of Modern Politics: Andrew Jackson, John Quincy Adams, and the Election of 1828* (New York: Oxford University Press, 2009); Robert V. Remini, *Martin Van Buren and the Making of the Democratic Party* (New York: W. W. Norton, 1951); Joel Silbey, *Martin Van Buren and the Emergence of American Popular Politics* (Lanham, Md.: Rowman & Littlefield, 2002).

27. Gerald Leonard, *The Invention of Party Politics: Federalism, Popular Sovereignty, and Constitutional Development in Illinois* (Chapel Hill: University of North Carolina Press, 2002), 175; Leonard, "Party as a 'Political Safeguard of Federalism,'" 221–81; Gerard N. Magliocca, *Andrew Jackson and the Constitution: The Rise and Fall of Generational Regimes* (Lawrence: University Press of Kansas, 2007); Robert V. Remini, *Andrew Jackson and the Bank War: A Study in the Growth of Presidential Power* (New York: W. W. Norton, 1967); Robert V. Remini, "The Constitution and the Presidencies: The Jackson Era," in *The Constitution and the American Presidency*, ed. Martin Fausold and Alan Shank (Albany: State University of New York Press, 1991), 29–44. See generally Harry L. Watson, *Liberty and Power: The Politics of Jacksonian America* (New York: Hill and Wang, 1990), and "Andrew Jackson and His Age," in Daniel Walker Howe, *What Hath God Wrought: The Transformation of America, 1815–1848* (New York: Oxford University Press, 2007), 328–66.

28. *National Party Platforms, 1840–1872*, 5th ed., ed. Donald Bruce Johnson and Kirk H. Porter (Urbana: University of Illinois Press, 1975), 3. Online: "Political Party Platforms of Parties Receiving Electoral Votes," in John Woolley and Gerhard Peters, The American Presidency Project. http://www.presidency.ucsb.edu/platforms.php [last consulted July 19, 2015].

29. Joel Silbey, "Organize, ORGANIZE, ORGANIZE!" in Silbey, *The American Political Nation, 1838–1893* (Stanford, Calif.: Stanford University

Press, 1991), 46–71. John Aldrich explains Jacksonian party organization from a theoretical perspective in *Why Parties?: The Origin and Transformation of Political Parties in America (Chicago: University of Chicago Press, 1995)*, 97–125.

30. Michael F. Holt, *Rise and Fall of the American Whig Party*, 15–18, 22–32. 83–87, 109–16, 684–86; Daniel Walker Howe, *The Political Culture of the American Whigs* (Chicago: University of Chicago Press, 1979); Howe, "The Whigs and Their Age," in Howe, *What Hath God Wrought*, 57–612.

31. Daniel Webster, Second Speech on Foot's Resolution [Reply to Hayne], in *The Writings and Speeches of Daniel Webster*, ed. J. W. McIntyre (Boston: Little, Brown and Co., 1903), 6: 3–75, quoted at 75.

32. Richard E. Ellis, *The Union at Risk: Jacksonian Democracy, States' Rights, and the Nullification Crisis* (New York: Oxford University Press, 1987); Daniel Walker Howe, "Battles Over Sovereignty," in Howe, *What Hath God Wrought*, 367–410.

33. Arthur M. Bestor, "The American Civil War as a Constitutional Crisis," *American Historical Review* 69 (January 1964): 327–52; Eric Foner, "Salmon P. Chase: The Constitution and the Slave Power," in *Free Soil, Free Labor, Free Men: The Ideology of the Republican Party Before the Civil War* (New York: Oxford University Press, 1970), 73–102; Don E. Fehrenbacher, *Slavery, Law, and Politics: The Dred Scott Case in Historical Perspective* (New York: Oxford University Press, 1981); Harold M. Hyman and William M. Wiecek, *Equal Justice Under Law: Constitutional Development, 1835–1875* (New York: Harper & Row, 1982); Magliocca, *Andrew Jackson and the Constitution*, 87–125.

34. For an excellent description of the process by which the Republican Party replaced the Whigs, and how the constitutional issues shifted from the economic ones that characterized the second party system to the slavery ones that characterized the third, from the perspective of a committed Whig, see Foner, *The Fiery Trial: Abraham Lincoln and American Slavery* (New York: W. W. Norton, 2010), 33–91.

35. Scott v. Sandford, 60 U.S. 393 (1857).

36. Bruce A. Ackerman, *We the People*, Vol. 2: *Transformations* (Cambridge, Mass.: Harvard University Press, 1998), 99–252; Michael Les Benedict, "Lincoln and Constitutional Politics," *Marquette Law Review* 93 (Summer 2010): 1,333–66; Michael Les Benedict, *A Compromise of Principle: Congressional Republicans and Reconstruction, 1863–1869* (New York: W. W. Norton, 1974); Michael Les Benedict, *Preserving the Constitution: Essays on Politics and the Constitution in the Reconstruction Era* (New York: Fordham University Press, 2006); Richard Franklin Bensel, *The Political Economy of American Industrial-*

ization, 1877–1900 (New York: Cambridge University Press, 2000) ; Richard Franklin Bensel, *Yankee Leviathan: The Origins of Central State Authority in America, 1859–1877* (New York: Cambridge University Press, 1990); Williamjames Hoffer, *To Enlarge the Machinery of Government: Congressional Debates and the Growth of the American State, 1858–1891* (Baltimore, Md.: Johns Hopkins University Press, 2007); Harold M. Hyman, *A More Perfect Union: The Impact of the Civil War and Reconstruction on the Constitution* (New York: Oxford University Press, 1973); Earl M. Maltz, *Civil Rights, the Constitution, and Congress, 1863–1869* (Lawrence: University Press of Kansas, 1990); Joel Silbey, *A Respectable Minority: The Democratic Party in the Civil War Era, 1860–1868* (New York: W. W. Norton, 1977) Peter Zavodnyik, *The Rise of the Federal Colossus: The Growth of Federal Power from Lincoln to FDR* (Santa Barbara, Cal.: Praeger, 2011), 45-247.

37. *National Party Platforms*, 38.

38. Michael Les Benedict, "Preserving Federalism: Reconstruction and the Waite Court," *The Supreme Court Review* 1978: 39–80; Pamela Brandwein, *Rethinking the Judicial Settlement of Reconstruction* (New York: Cambridge University Press, 2011).

39. Michael Les Benedict, "The Party, Going Strong: Congressional Elections in the Mid-Nineteenth Century," *Congress and the Presidency* 9 (Winter 1981–82): 37–60; Joel Silbey, "The Party State: Partisan Government in a Partisan Political Nation," in Silbey, *American Political Nation*, 176–95; Mark Wahlgren Summers, *Party Games*, 1–138.

40. See the People's Party's 1892 and 1896 national platforms in *National Campaign Platforms*, 89–91, 104–106; Busch, *Constitution on the Campaign Trail*, 161–62; Joel Silbey, "'When the Honor of the Country and the Vitality of Their Government Are at Stake': The System Ages," in Silbey, *American Political Nation*, 215–36; Gerard N. Magliocca, *The Tragedy of William Jennings Bryan: Constitutional Law and the Politics of Backlash* (New Haven, Conn.: Yale University Press, 2011), 28–47.

41. Michael Les Benedict, "Constitutional Politics in the Gilded Age," *Journal of the Gilded Age and Progressive Era* 9 (January 2010).

42. Howard Gillman, "How Political Parties Can Use the Courts to Advance Their Agendas: Federal Courts in the United States, 1875–1891," *American Political Science Review* 96 (September 2002): 511–524; Magliocca, *Tragedy of William Jennings Bryan*, 69–97; Arnold M. Paul, *Conservative Crisis and the Rule of Law: Attitudes of Bar and Bench, 1887–1895* (New York: Harper and Row, 1969); Mary Cornelia Porter, "'That Commerce Shall May Be Free': A New Look at the Old Laissez-Faire Court," *Supreme Court Review* 1979: 135–59.

43. *National Party Platforms*, 169.

44. Ibid., 176.

45. Ibid., 175, 176.

46. Ibid., 230.

47. John E. Semonche, *Charting the Future: The Supreme Court Responds to a Changing Society, 1890–1920* (Westport, Conn.: Greenwood Press, 1978); Alexander M. Bickel and Benno C. Schmidt, *The History of the Supreme Court*, Vol. 9: *The Judiciary and Responsible Government, 1910–1921* (New York: Macmillan, 1984); William F. Swindler, *Court and Constitution in the Twentieth Century*, Vol. 1: *The Old Legality* (Indianapolis: Bobbs-Merrill, 1969).

48. David Chalmers, *Hooded Americanism: The History of the Ku Klux Klan* (Garden City, N.Y.: Doubleday, 1965).

49. Franklin D. Roosevelt, "New Conditions Impose New Requirements upon Government and Those Who Conduct Government" [Campaign Address on Progressive Government at the Commonwealth Club, San Francisco, Calif., September 23, 1932], in *The Public Papers and Addresses of Franklin D. Roosevelt*, comp. Samuel I. Rosenman (New York: Random House, 1938), 1: 743–56, quoted at 754.

50. Paul Conkin, *FDR and the Origins of the Welfare State* (New York: Crowell, 1967); William E. Leuchtenburg, *Franklin Delano Roosevelt and the New Deal, 1932–1940* (New York: Harper and Row, 1963).

51. Richard A. Maidment, *The Judicial Response to the New Deal: The United States Supreme Court and Economic Regulation, 1934–1936* (Manchester, U.K., and New York: Manchester University Press, 1992); Jeff Shesol, *Supreme Power: Franklin Roosevelt vs. the Supreme Court* (New York: W. W. Norton, 1997); William F. Swindler, *Court and Constitution in the Twentieth Century*, Vol. 2: *The New Legality, 1932–1968* (Indianapolis: Bobbs-Merrill, 1970), 28–55.

52. *National Party Platforms*, 362.

53. Ibid., 365.

54. Franklin D. Roosevelt, "Fireside Chat on the Plan for the Reorganization of the Judiciary," in *Nothing to Fear: The Selected Addresses of Franklin Delano Roosevelt, 1932–1945*, ed. B. D. Zevin (New York: Houghton Mifflin, 1946), 98.

55. Barry Cushman, *Rethinking the New Deal Court: The Structure of a Constitutional Revolution* (New York: Oxford University Press, 1998); Patrick M. Garry, *An Entrenched Legacy: How the New Deal Constitutional*

Revolution Continues to Shape the Role of the Supreme Court (University Park: Pennsylvania State University Press, 2008); William E. Leuchtenburg, *The Supreme Court Reborn: The Constitutional Revolution in the Age of Roosevelt* (New York: Oxford University Press, 1995); Marilyn C. McKenna, *Franklin Roosevelt and the Great Constitutional War: The Court-Packing Crisis of 1937* (New York: Fordham University Press, 2002); Shesol, *Supreme Power*; Swindler, *Court and Constitution in the Twentieth Century*, 2: 56–80.

56. *National Party Platforms*, 487. See Matthew N. Beckman, *Pushing the Agenda: Presidential Leadership in U.S. Lawmaking, 1953–2004* (New York: Cambridge University Press, 2010); William E. Leuchtenburg, *In the Shadow of FDR: From Harry Truman to Barack Obama* (Ithaca, New York: Cornell University Press, 2009); Stephen Skowronek, *The Politics Presidents Make: Presidential Leadership from John Adams to Bill Clinton* (Cambridge, Mass.: Harvard University Press, 1993); Tushnet, "The President and National Party Politics," in *Why the Constitution Matters*, 41–57.

57. Angus Campbell et al., *The American Voter* (New York: John Wiley, 1960); Paul F. Lazarsfeld et al., *The People's Choice: How the Voter Makes Up His Mind in a Presidential Campaign*, 3rd ed. (New York: Columbia University Press, 1968). See David H. McKay, "The United States in Crisis: A Review of the American Political Science Literature," *Government and Opposition* 14 (Summer 1979): 373–85, and Benedict, "The Party, Going Strong," 47–49. On knowledge of the Constitution, see Busch, *Constitution on the Campaign Trail*, 208–213.

58. David M. Broder, *The Party's Over: The Failure of American Politics* (New York: Harper and Row, 1972); Walter Dean Burnham, "American Politics in the 1970s: Beyond Party?" in *The American Party System: Stages of Development*, ed. William Nisbet Chambers and Walter Dean Burnham (New York: Oxford University Press, 1975), 308–58; William J. Crotty, *American Parties in Decline* (Boston: Little, Brown, 1984); Doris A. Graber, *Mass Media and American Politics*, 8th ed. (Washington, D.C.: CQ Press, 2010); David Menefee-Libey, *The Triumph of Candidate-Centered Politics* (New York: Chatham House, 2000); Arthur M. Schlesinger, "Can the Party System Be Saved?" in *The American Constitutional System under Strong and Weak Parties*, ed. Patricia Bonomi et al. (New York: Praeger, 1981), 115–22; Martin P. Wattenberg, *The Rise of Candidate-Centered Politics: Presidential Elections in the 1980s* (Cambridge, Mass.: Harvard University Press, 1991); Martin P. Wattenberg, *The Decline of the Parties, 1951–1996* (Cambridge, Mass.: Harvard University Press, 1998).

59. Although the 1960s were once characterized as a period of decline in the New Deal partisan era, a number of analysts now see the establishment of a new partisan regime in those years. See, for example, Aldrich, *Why Parties?*,

260–66; Peter F. Nardulli, "Partisan Realignments and Electoral Independence: The Incidence, Distribution, and Magnitude of Enduring Electoral Change," in *Popular Efficacy in the Democratic Era: A Re-Examination of Electoral Accountability in the United States, 1828–2000* (Princeton, N.J.: Princeton University Press, 2005), 150–79. For constitutional issues in the Civil Rights partisan era, see Hugh Davis Graham, *The Civil Rights Era: Origins and Development of National Policy, 1960–1972* (New York: Oxford University Press, 1990); Nick Kotz, *Judgment Days: Lyndon Baines Johnson, Martin Luther King Jr., and the Laws that Changed America* (Boston: Houghton Mifflin, 2005); Donald G. Nieman, *Promises to Keep: African-Americans and the Constitutional Order, 1776 to the Present* (New York: Oxford University Press, 1991), 148–227; Sandra F. VanBurkleo, *"Belonging to the World": Women's Rights and American Constitutional Culture* (New York: Oxford University Press, 2001), 256–306; Sharon Whitney, *The Equal Rights Amendment: The History and the Movement* (Westport, Conn.: Greenwood Press, 1986).

60. *National Party Platforms*, 677.

61. 347 U.S. 483 (1954).

62. Ran Hirschl, "The Judicialization of Politics," in *Oxford Handbook of Law and Politics*, 119–41. See Lawrence Baum, "Supreme Court Activism and the Constitution," in *The Constitution and American Political Development*, ed. Peter F. Nardulli (Urbana: University of Illinois Press, 1992), 150–76; Melvin I. Urofsky, *The Continuity of Change: The Supreme Court and Individual Liberties, 1953–1986* (Belmont, Calif.: Wadsworth, 1989); Lucas A. Powe, Jr., *The Warren Court and American Politics* (Cambridge, Mass.: Harvard University Press, 2000).

63. Barry Friedman, "The Birth of an Academic Obsession: The History of the Countermajoritarian Difficulty, Part Five," *Yale Law Journal* 112 (November 2002): 153– 259; Laura Kalman, *The Strange Career of Legal Liberalism* (New Haven, Conn.: Yale University Press, 1996).

64. James Davison Hunter, *Culture Wars: The Struggle to Define America* (New York: Basic Books, 1991); Bruce Nesmith, *The New Republican Coalition: The Reagan Campaigns and White Evangelicals* (New York: P. Lang, 1994).

65. Thomas Byrne Edsall and Mary D. Edsall, *Chain Reaction: The Impact of Race, Rights, and Taxes on American Politics* (New York: W. W. Norton, 1992).

66. William C. Berman, *America's Right Turn: From Nixon to Bush* (Baltimore, Md.: Johns Hopkins University Press, 1994); Matthew Levendusky, *The Partisan Sort: How Liberals Became Democrats and Conservatives Became Republicans* (Chicago: University of Chicago Press, 2009);

Nicole Mellow, *The State of Disunion: Regional Sources of Modern American Partisanship* (Baltimore, Md.: Johns Hopkins University Press, 2008); Paul Pierson and Theda Skocpol, eds., *The Transformation of American Politics: Activist Government and the Rise of Conservatism* (Princeton, N.J.: Princeton University Press, 2007); Jeffrey M. Stonecash, *Political Parties Matter: Realignment and the Return of Partisan Voting* (Boulder, Colo.: Lynne Rienner Publications, 2006).

67. Republican Party Platform of 1980, in *Political Party Platforms, The American Presidency Project*, ed. John Woolley and Gerhard Peters (online: www.presidency.ucsb.edu.); Ronald Reagan, "Inaugural Address, January 20, 1981," ibid.

68. David L. Hudson, *The Rehnquist Court: Understanding Its Impact and Legacy* (Westport, Conn.: Praeger, 2007); Thomas Moylan Keck, *The Most Activist Supreme Court in History: The Road to Modern Judicial Conservatism* (Chicago: University of Chicago Press, 2004); Johnathan G. O'Neill, *Originalism in American Law and Politics: A Constitutional History* (Baltimore, Md.: Johns Hopkins University Press, 2005), 111–216; David G. Savage, *Turning Right: The Making of the Rehnquist Supreme Court* (New York: Wiley, 1993); Mark Tushnet, *A Court Divided: The Rehnquist Court and the Future of Constitutional Law* (New York: W. W. Norton, 2005).

69. Michael Patrick Leahy, *Covenant of Liberty: The Ideological Origins of the Tea Party Movement* (New York: Broadside Books, 2012).

70. 2012 Repubican Party Platform, in Political Party Platforms, The American Presidency Prjoject. http://www.presidency.ucsb.edu/ws/index.php?pid=101961) [accessed December 14, 2014].

71. 2008 Democratic Party Platform, ibid. http://www.presidency.ucsb.edu/ws/index.php?pid=78283; 2012 Democratic Party Platform, ibid. http://www.presidency.ucsb.edu/ws/index.php?pid=101962 [both accessed December 19, 2014].

72. See John Zvesper, "American Political Parties and Constitutional Government," in *Reflections on the Constitution: The American Constitution after Two Hundred Years*, ed. Richard Maidment and John Zvesper (Manchester, U.K.: Manchester University Press, 1989), 148–71. Zvesper considered the Constitution's anti-partyism as inhibiting the necessary presentation of alternatives in policy making and saw the inability of American parties to mobilize voters based on ideology as a weakness of the American political system.

73. Woodrow Wilson, *Constitutional Government in the United States* (New York: Columbia University Press, 1917; orig. pub. 1908), 204, 206.

74. John Gerring, *Party Ideologies in America, 1828–1996* (New York: Cambridge University Press, 1998). Although Gerring does not explicitly attend to the constitutional aspect of party ideologies, they emerge plainly from his analysis. For a more detailed account of the constitutional aspect of party divisions in American history, see chapter V.

75. Alan Abramowitz, *The Polarized Public? Why our Government is so Disfunctional* (Upper Saddle River, N.J.: Peaarson, 2013); Thomas E. Mann and Norman J. Ornstein, *It's Even Worse than It Looks: How the American Constitutional System Collided with the New Politics of Extremism* (New York: Basic Books, 2012).

76. For the Jacksonian "spoils system," see Michael F. Holt, *The Rise and Fall of the American Whig Party: Jacksonian Politics and the Onset of the Civil War* (New York: Oxford University Press, 1999), 414–18; Daniel Walker Howe, *What Hath God Wrought*, 331–34; Richard J. John, *Spreading the News: The American Postal System from Franklin to Morse* (Cambridge, Mass.: Harvard University Press, 1995), 206–40; Paul P. Van Riper, *History of the United States Civil Service* (Evanston, Ill.: Row, Peterson, 1958), 11–59.

77. The following discussion is based on Mark W. Summers, "Lincoln Spoils the War," in *Lincoln's Legacy: Ethics and Politics*, ed. Phillip Shaw Paludan (Urbana: University of Illinois Press, 2008), 30–47; Ari Hoogenboom, *Outlawing the Spoils: A History of the Civil Service Reform Movement, 1865–1883* (Urbana: University of Illinois Press, 1961); David J. Rothman, *Politics and Power: The United States Senate, 1869–1901* (New York: Atheneum,1969), 159–90; Van Riper, *History of the United States Civil Service*, 60–112; Stephen Skowronek, *Building a New American State: The Expansion of National Administrative Capacities, 1877–1920* (New York: Cambridge University Press, 1982), 47–84. For a nice, brief look at the operation of the Republican "machine" in Pennsylvania, see A. James Reichley, *The Life of the Parties: A History of American Political Parties* (New York: The Free Press, 1992), 157–58.

78. 53 U.S. Statutes at Large 1147 (1939). For the steady elimination of patronage in the federal civil service after 1883, see David A. Schultz and Robert Maranto, *The Politics of Civil Service Reform* (New York: Peter Lang, 1988), 87–99; Skowronek, *Building a New American State*, 177–211.

79. Rutan v. Republican Party of Illinois, 497 U.S. 62 (1990).

80. Anne Freeman, *Patronage: An American Tradition* (Chicago: Nelson-Hall, 1994), 168–83.

81. For political practices in the nineteenth century, see Glenn C. Altschuler and Stuart M. Blumin, *Rude Republic: Americans and Their Politics in the Nineteenth Century* (Princeton, N.J.: Princeton University

Press, 2000); Michael Les Benedict, "The Party, Going Strong," 37–60;
Richard F. Bensel, *The American Ballot Box in the Mid-Nineteenth Century*
(New York: Cambridge University Press, 2004); Dinkin, *Campaigning in
America*, 31–93; John McClymer et al., "Public Speaking in an Outspoken
Age: Oratory in 19th Century America," E Pluribus Unum *Project: America
in the 1770s, 1850s, and 1920s*, online at http://www1.assumption.edu/
ahc/rhetoric/oratory.html; Mark W. Summers, *Party Games: Getting,
Keeping, and Using Power in Gilded Age Politics* (Chapel Hill: University of
North Carolina Press, 2004).

    82. Candidates at the highest level reflected this change, as they stressed
their humble origins. Andrew Jackson had been born in a log cabin. The
patrician Whig candidate for president in 1840, William Henry Harrison,
supposedly shared Jackson's log-cabin origins and was a devotee of hard
cider as well. Abraham Lincoln had been a rail-splitter. President Andrew
Johnson stressed his background as a Tennessee tailor. Ulysses Grant had
been a tanner. Massachusetts senator and U.S. vice president Henry Wilson
was a shoemaker. See Edward Pessen, *The Log Cabin Myth: The Social
Backgrounds of American Presidents* (New Haven, Conn.: Yale University
Press, 1984). Myth is not always fiction, though. For Abraham Lincoln's
humble origins and how politics provided his opportunity for social
advancement, "as with so many contemporaries in Jacksonian America"
(37), see Eric Foner, *The Fiery Trial*, 35–37.

    83. Michael Les Benedict, "Lincoln and Constitutional Politics";
Benedict, "Constitutional Politics in the Gilded Age," 7–35; Morton Keller,
The Art and Politics of Thomas Nast (New York: Oxford University Press,
1968); Carolyn Steward Dyer, *Political Patronage of the Wisconsin Press,
1849–1860: New Perspectives on the Economics of Patronage* (Columbia,
S.C.: Association for Education in Journalism and Mass Communica-
tion, University of South Carolina, College of Journalism, 1989); Mark
W. Summers, *The Press Gang: Newspapers and Politics, 1865–1878* (Chapel
Hill: University of North Carolina Press, 1994). Note the campaign
manuals published semi-annually by Edward McPherson from 1868 to
1894, titled *A Political Manual for . . .* [1866–1869] (Washington, D.C.:
Philp and Solomons, 1866–1869), followed by *A Hand-Book of Politics for*
[the relevant year] (Washington, D.C.: Philp and Solomons, 1870–1894).

    84. For the rise of independent journalism, see Ted Curtis, *The Gilded
Age Press, 1865–1900* (Westport, Conn.: Praeger, 2003). For twentieth-
and twenty-first-century developments, see Michael M. Franz et al., eds.,
Campaign Advertising and American Democracy (Philadelphia: Temple
University Press, 2007); Graber, *Mass Media and American Politics*; Dinkin,

Campaigning in America, 159–98. For the effect on public understanding of the issues, see the works cited in note 57 above.

85. Arthur C. Paulson, *Realignment and Party Revival: Understanding American Electoral Politics at the Turn of the Twenty-First Century* (Westport, Conn.: Praeger, 2000), 148–322.

86. Writing about the Albany Regency's creation of the first thorough patronage system in New York in the 1810s and 1820s, Robert Remini observed, "It was not so much the rewarding of partisans and the mass lopping off of rebellious heads that explained Regency success as it was the skilful, highly judicious manner in which the power was exercised." He noted how "carefully . . . the members consider[ed] the prejudices and feelings of local communities to be affected by their appointments" and how "thoroughly . . . they investigate[d] the many and petty details connected with the distribution of the patronage." Robert V. Remini, *Martin Van Buren and the Making of the Democratic Party* (New York: W. W. Norton, 1951), 9. The papers of U.S. senators in the Library of Congress and elsewhere are filled with examples. For instance, even after Congress passed the Civil Service Reform Act, which protected officeholders against partisan removal, Wisconsin senator Thomas C. Spooner struggled with the nomination of a postmaster. "I want you people to get together upon this question if it is possible," he wrote a local officeholder. "We cannot afford to have a split and fight in our own ranks in that district. It is against the party interest, and I think I am entitled to an honest attempt on the part of you leading, working Republicans to harmonize, and to enable me to recommend on whose appointment will give general satisfaction." Spooner to S. B. Stanchfield, January 25, 1890, quoted in Spooner to O. C. Steenberg, February 10, 1890, Spooner Papers, Manuscripts Division, Library of Congress, Washington, D.C.

87. Hoogenboom, *Outlawing the Spoils*; Stephen Skowronek, *Building a New American State*, 47–84, 177–211.

88. David Brady, "The Party System in the House of Representatives," in *Parties and Politics in American History*, ed. L. Sandy Maisel and William G. Shade (New York: Garland, 1994), 188. The great political scientist V. O. Key suggested the American party system was even more decentralized than one would expect in a federal system. "Federalism in our formal governmental machinery includes a national element independent of the states, but in our party organization the independent and national element is missing. Party structure is more nearly confederate than federal in nature," he wrote. V. O. Key, Jr., *Politics, Parties, and Pressure Groups* (New York: Crowell, 1964), 334.

89. James S. Chase, *Emergence of the Presidential Nominating Convention 1789–1832* (Urbana: University of Illinois Press, 1973); Daniel Klinghard, "Localism and the Jacksonian Mode," in *The Nationalization of American Political Parties, 1880–1896* (New York: Cambridge University Press, 2010), 25–65; John F. Reynolds, "The Search for Harmony: The Convention System in the Party Period," in *The Demise of the American Convention System, 1880–1911* (New York: Cambridge University Press, 2006), 18–61.

90. Klinghard, *The Nationalization of American Political Parties*, 98–234; Nelson W. Polsby and Aaron B. Wildavsky, *Presidential Elections: Strategies and Structures of American Politics* (New York: Chatham House, 2000), 46–48.

91. For the importance of state-by-state primary elections to the presidential nomination, see Wildavsky, *Presidential Elections*, 98–150.

92. The following discussion is based on the works cited in note 28 above.

93. David E. Lewis, *The Politics of Presidential Appointments: Political Control and Bureaucratic Performance* (Princeton, N.J.: Princeton University Press, 2008); Sarah A. Binder, *Advice & Dissent: The Struggle to Shape the Federal Judiciary* (Washington, D.C.: Brookings Institution Press, 2009); Amy Steigerwalt, *Battle Over the Bench: Senators, Interest Groups, and Lower Court Confirmations* (Charlottesville: University of Virginia Press, 2010).

94. See, for example, Samuel Issacharoff and Richard H. Pildes, "Politics as Markets: Partisan Lockups of the Democratic Process," *Stanford Law Review* 50 (February 1998): 643–717.

95. Ex parte Yarbrough, 110 U.S. 651 (1884); United States v. Classic, 313 U.S. 299 (1941); Nixon v. Herndon, 273 U.S. 536 (1927); Smith v. Allwright, 321 U.S. 649 (1944).

96. The following discussion is based on Paul Beck and Marjorie Randon Hershey, *Party Politics in America*, 9th ed. (New York: Longman, 2000), 56–58; John Epperson, *The Changing Legal Status of Parties in the United States* (New York: Garland, 1986); Leon D. Epstein, *Political Parties in the American Mold* (Madison: University of Wisconsin Press, 1986), 155–99; Hoogenboom, *Outlawing the Spoils*; Skowronek, *Building a New American State*, 47–84, 177–211; Reynolds, *The Demise of the American Convention System*, 105–236; Alan Ware, *The American Direct Primary: Party Institutionalization and Transformation in the North* (New York: Cambridge University Press, 2002).

97. Sidney M. Milkis, *Political Parties and Constitutional Government: Remaking American Democracy* (Baltimore, Md.: Johns Hopkins University Press, 1999), 42.

98. Adam Winkler, "Voters' Rights and Parties' Wrongs: Political Party Regulation in the Courts, 1886–1915," *Columbia Law Review* 100 (April 2000): 873–99, quoted at 878; Epperson, *Changing Legal Status of Political Parties*, 63–81, quoted at 80.

99. Zephyr Teachout, *Corruption in America: From Benjamin Franklin's Snuffbox to Citizens United* (Cambridge, Mass.: Harvard University Press, 2014), 188–94.

100. 86 U.S. Statutes at Large 3 (1972).

101. Robert B. Hawkins, Jr., and John Shannon, *The Transformation in American Politics: Implications for Federalism* (Washington, D.C.: Advisory Commission on Intergovernmental Relations, 1987); *Campaigns and Elections American Style: Transforming American Politics*, ed. James A. Thurber and Candice J. Nelson, 4th ed. (Boulder, Colo.: Westview Press, 2014). For an overview of campaign finance reform, see R. Sam Garrett, "Money, Politics, and Policy: Campaign Finance Before and After Citizens United," ibid, 77–99.

102. Buckley v. Valeo, 424 U.S. 1 (1976).

103. Colorado Republican Federal Campaign Committee v. FEC, 518 U.S. 604 (1996).

104. FEC v. Colorado Republican Federal Campaign Committee, 433 U.S. 531 (2001).

105. A. James Reichley, *Life of the Parties*, 353–81.

106. Paul Beck and Marjorie Randon Hershey, *Party Politics in America*, 9th ed. (New York: Longman, 2000), 250.

107. Bipartisan Campaign Reform Act (McCain-Feingold Act), U.S. Statutes at Large 116 (2002): 81.

108. McConnell v. FEC, 540 U.S. 93 (2003); Citizens United v. FEC, 558 U.S. 310 (2010).

109. SpeechNow.org v. FEC, 599 F.3d 686 (D.C. Cir. 2010).

110. American Tradition Partnership v. Bullock, 132 S. Ct. 2490 (2012).

111. Nicholas Confessore, "Lines Blurring Between PACs and Candidates," *New York Times*, August 28, 2011, p. 1.

112. Michael S. Kang, "The Year of the Super PAC," *George Washington Law Review* 81 (November 2013): 1902-27; Derek Willis, "The Special Powers of SuperPACS, Not Just for Federal Elections," *New York Times* (online), December 8, 2014. http://www.nytimes.com/2014/12/09/upshot/the-special-powers-of-super-pacs-and-not-just-for-federal-elections.

html?emc=eta1&abt=0002&abg=1 [consulted December 10, 2014]; Derek Willis, "Outside Groups Set Spending Record in Midterms," ibid., December 11, 2014. http://www.nytimes.com/2014/12/11/upshot/outside-groups-set-spending-record-in-midterms-.html?emc=eta1&abt=0002&abg=1 [consulted Dec. 10, 2014] Eric Lichtblau and Nicholas Confessore, "What Campaign Filings Won't Show: Super PACs' Growing Sway," ibid., July 15, 2015. http://www.nytimes.com/2015/07/16/us/politics/election-2016-fundraising-campaign-filings.html?emc=eta1&_r=0 [consulted July 18, 2015].

113. Tari Renner, "Political Parties—Beyond Revitalization," in Campaigns on the Cutting Edge, ed. Richard J. Semiatin, 2d ed. (Los Angeles, Cal.: CQ Press, 2013), 103–20.

114. Kang, "The Year of the Super PAC."

115. Politics: Election 2012, "Independent Spending Totals," *New York Times*, Politics: Election 2012 at http://elections.nytimes.com/2012/campaign-finance/independent-expenditures/totals. While some commentators implied that the failure of mainly Republican super PACs to carry the presidential and senate elections would diminish their future influence, that seems unlikely. See Nicholas Confessore, "Result Won't Limit Campaign Money Any More than Ruling Did," *New York Times*, November 11, 2012 at http://www.nytimes.com/2012/11/12/us/politics/a-vote-for-unlimited-campaign-financing.html?ref=campaignfinance&_r=0 (both articles last consulted November 10, 2014).

116. On the conflict from a perspective sympathetic to the extreme conservative, or Tea-Party, insurgents, see Ronald T. Libby, *Purging the Republican Party: Tea Party Campaigns and Elections* (Lanham, Md.: Lexington Books, 2014). See Alan I. Abramowitz, "Not Their Cup of Tea: The Republican Establishment Versus the Tea Party," November 15, 2013, Sabato's Crystal Ball, University of Virginia Center for Politics. http://www.centerforpolitics.org/crystalball/articles/not-their-cup-of-tea-the-republican-establishment-versus-the-tea-party [accessed December 15, 2014]; David Levinthal, "GOP Civil War Rages in Senate Primary Battles," May 8, 2014, Center for Public Integrity. http://www.publicintegrity.org/2014/05/08/14732 [accessed December 15, 2014].

117. Nixon v. Condon, 286 U.S. 73 (1932); Smith v. Allright, 321 U.S. 649 (1944).

118. Michael A. Fitts, "Back to the Future: The Enduring Dilemmas Revealed in the Supreme Court's Treatment of Political Parties," in *The U.S. Supreme Court and the Political Process*, 2nd ed., ed. David K. Ryden (Washington, D.C.: Georgetown University Press, 2002), 97–111; Paul R.

Petterson, "Partisan Autonomy or State Regulatory Authority? The Court as Mediator," ibid., 112–25; Cynthia Grant Bowman, "The Supreme Court's Patronage Decisions and the Theory and Practice of Politics," ibid., 126–43.

119. Cousins v. Wigoda, 419 U.S. 477 (1975); Democratic Party v. Wisconsin ex rel. La Follette, 450 U.S. 107 (1981). See Epstein, *Political Parties in an American Mold*, 189–97.

120. Tashjian v. Republican Party, 479 U.S. 208 (1986); California Democratic Party v. Jones, 530 U.S. 567 (2000); Eu v. San Francisco Democratic Committee, 489 U.S. 214 (1989); Timmons v. Twin Cities Area New Party, 520 U.S. 351 (1997). See Benjamin D. Black, "Developments in the State Regulation of Major and Minor Political Parties," *Cornell Law Review* 82 (November 1996): 109–81; John C. Green, "The Right to Party: The United States Supreme Court and Contemporary Political Parties," in *Superintending Democracy: The Courts and the Political Process*, ed. Christopher P. Banks and John C. Green (Akron, Ohio: University of Akron Press, 2001), 149–62.

121. Epstein, *Political Parties in the American Mold*, 180–84.

122. McConnell v. FEC, at 144–45.

123. Ibid., 352. Justice Anthony M. Kennedy also criticized the law for legislating a preference for "corporate media" over political parties in the political process. Ibid., 286.

124. Robert C. Post, *Citizens Divided: Campaign Reform and the Constitution* (Cambridge, Mass.: Harvard University Press, 2014),

125. Teachout, *Corruption in America*, 241.